RABBITS AND RESILIENCE

Mark Ayckbourn

Dedication

I would like to express my deepest gratitude to all those who have been a part of my journey, from cherished childhood friends to new friends I've met along the way. You guys have given me so much support and guidance, even when you didn't know you were doing it.

To my Wife (not Wife) Ruth and my daughter Danni, thank you. Without you two and your love, I would probably be in a hotel room alone or a pub somewhere, wondering where the truth of my story would land. You made me the man I am today.

My Mum, you have been by my side through every step. You are the only person I could truly open up to, no matter what happened. You are an amazing lady, Granny Paddy!

My Brother, Gary, I've spent more time with you than anyone in my life and spoken to you more times a day than is healthy. We did well, and we have been a great team.

To you, dear reader, and my future family through the generations, I hope you enjoy the journey through my first 45 years... remember:

Attitude is Everything – Leave Nothing to Regret!

About the Author

My name is Mark Ayckbourn. I've travelled the world and seen so many things. I've been blessed with my amazing family. I've seen money come and go and realised how little it defines you. I've been up in the air and on the bones of my backside. I've been happy, and I've been devastated. I've loved, I've lost, and I've learned valuable life lessons along the way.

I have looked death straight in the eye and learned to appreciate life. I don't suffer fools. But I will give a chance where a chance needs to be given. I like a twist of optimism. You see? Try to see the bright side. Pay it forward. They say we change throughout our lives. And that's okay, As long as you remember the versions of yourself that you used to be.

My name means almost the same as it did a thousand years ago. Of Mars. Spartan, almost. You could say it means strong in times of adversity, but I'll leave that to the stories.

I want to tell you *my* story.

Table of Contents

Introduction

No two stories are ever quite the same. No one has lived your experiences. Or mine. Everyone has a tale to tell. So much has happened throughout my life that I feel the urge to share. Welcome to the beautifully wild and weird story of my life so far. I believe that no one is a sinner, and no one is a saint.

People follow their life path and have no actual knowledge of where it may take them. What is true is that life's a crazy blur, where we live on the edge of our own stories. And this one's mine.

Unfortunately for you, as I share a medley of tales intriguing enough to ruffle some feathers if every detail were told, for now, many side stories must be hidden away for discretion. Although some have given me many sleepless nights or the biggest laughs, this is not the book for it... you can just wait for book two!

Everyone makes decisions for their own reasons, and I disagree with many of them. But that is why the world is so unique—people can do the strangest things!

With time, or perhaps over a beer or two, I might be persuaded to reveal the secrets behind these stories. So, stay tuned, and if curiosity really gets the better of you, ask me when no one else is listening.

This is a tale of resilience, heartbreak, growing pains, success, and failure—oh, and a multi-million-dollar lawsuit and a whole lot of Rampant Rabbits—but we'll get to that later.

Chapter 1

Fractured Families on Curlew Drive

My memories started when I was around five years old, as my family went through a tough breakup. My Mum left, and what made it more complicated was that she left with a good friend of the family, a neighbour.

I don't remember a lot about my early years, but one thing is for sure: our house wasn't a very happy place. My Mum and Dad argued a lot, and as a young boy, I often found myself hiding at the top of the stairs, listening to them argue and crying quietly. I vividly remember looking through the curved bars of our bannister, something similar to a musical clef, watching as my Mum stood doing the ironing in our living room downstairs while Dad was standing opposite, both shouting at each other. I had no idea what they were arguing about, but I remember feeling cold. Confusion as their voices got louder and the tone more harsh than the moment before. I want to get involved and stop it, but I am frozen to the spot, just listening to the noise.

When I was only five, my Mum decided to leave. Her heart was interested in a neighbour from six doors away, and her leaving left a big gap in our lives and caused the whole neighbourhood to get involved. Before this, we all holidayed together and spent evenings and weekends around each other's houses, so this was a fracture that would never heal in Curlew Drive.

My brothers, Gary and Mike, felt the changes too, but in their own ways. I was too young to understand everything, but I could tell something was wrong. They were both much older, so it's hard for me to remember exactly how they reacted, but as the years passed, I realised that neither of them had dealt with it properly.

It's hard at such a young age to understand what's happening, but as the years went by and my mind matured, I came to empathise with both my Mum and Dad. Mum clearly wanted out of the relationship, and she had her reasons.Dad wasn't always the easiest to get on with. He was stubborn, and after so many years together and three children, people grow apart

Nevertheless, Dad was left mortally hurt and humiliated. His Wife and mother of their three boys leaving him for a family friend must have been horrifying. Everyone in the whole neighbourhood knew, meaning every time he left our house, he could feel the whispers from friends and strangers alike.

Me and Dad (Pops)

Chapter 2

Crossroads Between Love and Loss

In those crazy years, court became a sort of routine for us. It wasn't a joyful ride but a rollercoaster of legal jargon and grown-up problems that a kid shouldn't have had to deal with. The legal dance started because my parents couldn't see eye to eye, and we unwittingly became pawns in this game of family chess.

Things were different back then. It might have been rare for a dad to go all-in for custody in Great Britain. People raised their eyebrows and whispered about it as if it broke some unwritten rule.

"Why do you want to live with your dad?" folks would ask me. It wasn't rocket science. I just wanted to be with my brothers, Gary and Mike. Those two were my anchors, my go-to guys when life got topsy-turvy.

They were also the two who took me places and made sure that when our parents were fighting, I wouldn't be around to see it.

The court saga kicked into gear when I was barely old enough to tie my shoelaces—six or seven, to be exact. It wasn't some playground squabble; it was a full-blown family feud, and Mum and Dad were the main event. They both wanted me to live with them, so they decided to let a judge referee our domestic showdown.

Courtrooms turned into this strange battleground. It wasn't about toys or games but about where I should lay my head each night. Every time we stepped into that legal arena, it felt like we were entering a realm where somebody else had complete control over all our lives. How could it be that someone who knows nothing about you can decide where you live? As an adult, I understand the process and see that it may be the only way for two people who are so passionate, stubborn, and loving to agree. Still, at the time, you are dragged between your family and houses like a discarded teddy bear.

I remember being at school one day when my friend Neil came up to me saying that his family had watched my Mum on TV the day before, talking about how bad my Dad was and showing her frustration with the UK system. At this point, my personal life wasn't personal anymore; everyone knew what was happening, and everyone knew every detail of my life. Every evening before bed for over five years, I had to pack my bag for the next day. Every night, I alternated between both houses, so I had no stability and nowhere did I really feel at home.

Although I was loved; .loved so much that they fought for me for many years. I felt the love and saw it in their actions towards me, but it still didn't stop the feeling of being the knot in the middle of a tug-of-war.

Chapter 3

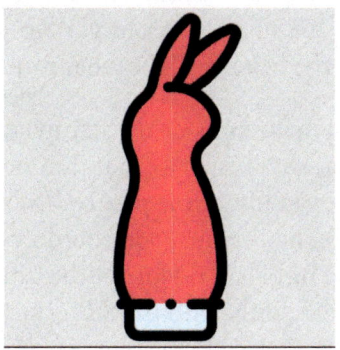

Once They're Gone, They're Gone.

Losing people we love is something everyone goes through, and when I was a young teenager, I felt really sad saying goodbye to my Granny, who was my Mum's Mum. She was an amazing Granny, like a super special lady, and she was a bit quirky and crazy, just like my Mum. I still remember all the cool things about her, including our trips to McDonalds together, and those memories still mean the world to me.

Granny was like the boss of our family in Catholic West Belfast. They were known for being super funny, probably some of the funniest people I've ever met. Family was super important to them. After half of them moved to Fulham, London, my Granny's house was always lively. There were card games, bets on horses, black & white country and western films on the TV and lots of good times. I can still picture my Uncle George, a very large guy, sitting in his pants on the sofa watching the horses, 'effing and blinding' when it romped home in last place. It felt like a place where everyone belonged and shared good family moments.

My uncles were always around, making the house feel really welcoming. All the laughter, talking, and dishes clinking together made it seem like a happy place. It was like a big family, connected by love, beer, and a shared history.

On the other side of my family, my Pops (My Dad's dad) was like a kind hero. He used to be a chef in the army, and he made the best roast potatoes EVER. I can still remember how crispy and delicious they were. He was really good at turning simple ingredients into incredible meals and always made me feel welcome. His was a quiet house, the opposite to my Granny's, but I loved playing in his small, bricked garden, kicking a half inflated plastic football against the brick wall for what must have been hours.

On the other hand, my memories of my nanny are very different. For as long as I can remember, she wasn't well, and in my childhood memories, she stayed in her chair, watching time pass by. I remember my Pops being super caring and feeding her because she couldn't do it herself. It showed how much he loved her, but I had no idea at the time how this scene would be replayed later in my life, only with my father sitting in the chair.

Even though these memories are a bit sad, I still hold onto the good times I had with my Granny and Pops. Those moments were filled with love, laughter, and tasty meals. Even though they're not here anymore, their passion still stays with me. Losing them taught me how powerful love is and how remarkable people can leave lasting memories in our hearts.

Chapter 4

Shadows and Strength

The whole legal tango dragged on and on for what felt like an eternity, shadowing me until I was fourteen. Both my parents were amazing to me. They sacrificed so much to ensure I had everything I needed, but I grew up knowing I never wanted a 'broken home' for my children. No matter what happened, I knew I wanted one happy home for my family.

Those court battles weren't just about boring legal mumbo-jumbo. Oh no, they brought a truckload of stress and problems for all of us. The court held the magical power to decide where I should call home, and every trip to those hallowed legal halls was a rollercoaster of emotions. The decisions made in those courtrooms had the potential to turn our lives upside down, like a game-changing move on a giant chessboard we never signed up for.

I remember the quiet talks between the lawyers, the serious faces of the judge, and the nervous feeling in the air every time we went into the courtroom. It was a world of complicated words and arguments, and as a kid caught in the middle, I didn't really understand any of it.

But my Dad was like a strong guide. At a time when people usually thought moms should get custody, my Dad fought against that idea. He went to every court hearing, believing that dads could be just as good at caring for their kids.

The court battles were tough for all of us. Emotions were high, and it put a strain on our relationships. My Mum, who loved me, was stuck in a kind of fight that none of us wanted. On the other hand, my Dad took on the responsibility with a strong determination, trying to make things feel normal for us, his kids.

Dad lost out on his life, with no trips to the pub or nights out; he played the role of Dad and Mum together. Mum, on the other, had been clearly finding it all unbearable, and I know she tried a couple of times to take her own life. It must have been horrific for her, especially as Gary and Mike sided with our Dad. She must have felt so lonely, so helpless. Wanting to turn back the hands of time and was full of regret for the pain she could see on her children's faces.

I know that certain universities in the UK actually went on to teach about our own personal custody to their legal students, learning how 'not' to do divorce and custody proceedings.

Gary moved out when I was around eight or nine, but Mike stuck around until I was sixteen or seventeen. Our family went through a tough time when our parents decided not to stay together anymore, and things changed a lot.

After our parents split up, Gary and Mike decided they didn't want to see or talk to Mum anymore. They blamed her solely and wanted to keep away from family issues. But for me, it was different. I wanted to spend time with Mum, but at the same time, I really loved being with my brothers at Dad's home, my home.

Every day, after school, I would go to a different house. One day I'd be at Dad's place; the next, I'd be at Mum's, and it kept going like that.

Every few months, a person from the court would visit and ask me where I wanted to live. Every time, I said the same thing: "I want to live with my brothers." In the end, the court decided I should stay with Dad, mainly because they thought Mum was responsible for the family breaking apart. Even though Mum and Dad both loved me a lot, my heart was set on being with my older brothers, who were like my strong support.

Mum's new partner was called Richard, although I only ever called him "Titch" because he was 6" 4 and I thought I was being funny. Dad also found friendship that led to a long-life partner in Ann, and we now fondly call her "Nanny Ann." Both couples grew old together. Looking back, it seems like they went separate ways and started new families, which was the right thing for everyone.

Please bear with me as I fast-forward a few years, as it is unfair to leave the relationships as above. Although both Gary and Mike had refused a relationship with our Mum for many years, everything changed the moment they had children of their own. When Gary and Delph had Bethyn and Mike and Sian had Jack, a switch changed within them. Both, in their own time, picked up the phone to Mum and welcomed her back into their lives.

I had never left Mum; she had been amazing to me throughout, and as the years passed, I talked more about her. How fantastic our relationship was, how kind and loving she was, and also how regretful.

Mikee, Mum, Gary and Me

I'm so happy my brothers opened the door for our Mum to become a Granny for her grandchildren (Gary with Ben, Bethyn and Ciara & Mike with Conor, Alex & Jack).

Although they welcomed her back, there was always an unspoken distance. But remember, they also blamed Dad, especially as they grew older and understood that it takes two to tango (normally!)

I can only thank the stars that I was too young to understand everything and, therefore, had a fantastic relationship with both of them throughout my life.

Chapter 5

Bonded by Friendship

When I was a kid, my best friend was Matt Barton. Our families were really close. Matt's Mum, Sue, was my Mum's best friend, and they both helped each other through so much sadness and heartache.

Matt's older brothers and sister were friends with my brothers, Gary and Mike. So, we were like two families that were always together. Even now, we are close. My daughter Danni is a good mate of Matt's boy Ollie, Andy's two girls, Paul's boys, and Sarah's children. Our two families are joined in so many ways. We are part of theirs, and they are ours forever.

Matt and I did everything together – holidays, sleepovers, you name it. Even when my Mum moved out, she moved in with Sue (Matts's Mum) on the same street as our family home, 50 yards from our front door. It was all a bit weird.

Matt and I were super close. We faced all kinds of things together. When things got tough for my family, I even stayed with Matt's family at Sue's house during some legal stuff. It was strange because my Dad and brothers still lived really close, just down the road.

We spent hours and hours sitting on his front drive racing small toy cars down the slope and into the road (thankfully, back then, there weren't many cars about!). The car that made it furthest won. I still have my winning 'dream team' cars at Mum's house; they hold something special to me.

No matter what game we played, Matt always ended up hurt or injured. One time, while racing our bikes throughout the neighbourhood streets, his brakes failed, shooting him down the hill, over the road junction, and directly through a glass door of our neighbour. Matt was virtually unhurt, but I still remember for a split second as he went out of sight that I was going to have to tell Sue that he was a goner!!

Another time, we were in my living room playing 'keepy-uppy' with a balloon, and Matt suddenly shouted 'Ahh'; he looked down at his foot and nothing, so he carried on. 30 seconds later, I could see his white sock was completely red, with blood pouring out.

He had stood on a Swisse army knife that someone had left on the floor, and it pieced the sole of his foot – 3 hours at A&E and several stitches later, we were back at it again!

Then, when we were about 12 or 13, something terrible happened. I remember Matt was with me at Mum and Titch's house when we heard that Matt's Dad, Mac, had passed away.

It was really sad. Matt was naturally shocked and upset, and there wasn't anything anyone could do to make it better. I tried to help him feel better, but it was tough. Seeing how much Matt hurt made my problems seem unimportant.

I didn't know Matt's Dad, Mac, personally, but both Dad and Mum always said he was a good guy. When Mac passed away, I wished I knew him, wished things were different.

Titch with Graeme Meikle, Simon Holloway, Matt Barton, Me, Alan Meikle, Neil Holloway

It was a sorrowful time for both of our families as we tried to deal with the aftermath of such a terrible loss.

Chapter 6

Burred Memories of Self-Discovery

I t wasn't until I hit my late teens and twenties that I realised just how tough those years had been. It's weird, but I can only remember a few things from when I was five to around eighteen. I couldn't even recall the good times playing football with my friends at Barton Rovers. It's like many of those memories were hidden from me by my brain to protect me in the future.

Back in the day, if you looked at me from the outside, you'd see a super-confident and happy guy. I had a bunch of great friends, and life was a blast. People wanted to be around me, and I knew I had teenage charm because, by the time I hit 13, I was friends with every group in the school, including teachers and parents and was the most successful guy with girls.

Looking back, I'm not exactly proud of it, but I didn't know anything different back then. Every day and night I headed out, I'd manage to find a new girl. Every holiday brought more girlfriends than there were days in the trip, more stories than I could remember, and more risk-taking than you could imagine. In fact, I was such an arse that I started writing a list because I couldn't keep track of how many girls and what happened with them. That list quickly turned into a book, believe it or not.

It wasn't just about impressing girls. It was also about the great times and adventures I had with my mates, Alan, Garthy, and Bones. These guys weren't just friends but the best mates you'd want around for every good and bad moment.

Even though Bones and Garthy got serious with Cathy and Sarah in their teens, they still hung out with me. We stuck together through everything, making sure our nights out were full of laughter and exciting stories we never remembered because we were normally so drunk.

In my later teenage years, my Dad and Ann spent most weekends in their caravan in Southsea, meaning I had full access to a free home (with only Mike for company, and he was out more than me).

Nanny Ann, Pops, Danni and Me

My nights were spent going out, meeting a girl, and taking her home. Mike and I would always chuckle when the two strange girls met first thing the following morning.

Alan, Garthy, Bones, and I formed a strong bond that lasted beyond the moment. We had carefree nights, made spontaneous decisions, and had a lot of exciting opportunities, usually involving several other mates I would still speak to today. Only last week, a mate I hadn't seen in a very long time reminisced about a story of him and me in Tenerife with a couple of girls... Honestly, I don't remember, but I chucked along with him just to see where the story went – it sounded like the three of us had a blast!!

Bones, Alan, Me and Garthy

We would just jump in a car and drive to another town or down to the coast at Southsea so Dad could buy us a few drinks at the holiday camp bar before we went to the seafront clubs to pick up even more girls.

We went through the ups and downs of growing up together, creating memories that still make me smile today. Some things we did back then make me cringe, but that's all part of growing up, right?

These mates were like partners in crime, sharing stories that would become a big part of our history. Alan, with his quick wit and risk-taking attitude, could turn any regular night into a remarkable tale. Bones, always up for an adventure, added excitement to our escapades. And Garthy, the more reliable one, managed to keep us on the right side of the law while still being the life of the party—with the best dance moves!

Those were the days of not worrying too much, where every night held the promise of something great. The memories of those times have stuck with me, becoming treasured moments from the past. Remember, we never had cameras or mobile phones, so it was all about the storytelling the following morning. Looking back, I can't help but smile at the simplicity of those moments, the laughter filling the air, and the shared understanding that these friendships shared stories that will fill a lifetime.

Sure, some of the things we did back then might make me squirm now, but they were essential parts of our growing up story. In the end, it wasn't just about getting older; it was about getting older together and having a giggle along the way.

Chapter 7

Spreading my Wings

In my early twenties, life was filled with excitement and opportunity. I had everything a young adult could desire—money, space, freedom, and a tight-knit circle of friends who were always up for an adventure. But when I thought everything was cruising smoothly, an unexpected twist rocked my world.

It was an ordinary day until my Pops dropped a bombshell that reverberated through the very foundation of my existence. "I am moving to Spain... I've brought a house with Ann and sold this place. You have three months to find somewhere to live," he announced casually as if he hadn't just upended my entire life.

"Really, Dad?! What the hell?" I exclaimed, disbelief coursing through every fibre of my being. It was a curveball I never saw coming, and I was scrambling to figure out my next move.

In a frantic bid to regain stability, I immediately contacted Garthy, my closest confidant and partner-in-crime, to share the news. With unwavering determination, we embarked on a house-hunting spree fueled by the prospect of newfound independence and the chance to carve out a place of our own in the world.

House Buddies: Garth (Gareth Fullbrook), Bones (Tony Walls) and Me. Also, Gregzy (Simon Gregory), not a housemate but a long-term friend

However, our lofty aspirations quickly collided with the harsh realities of our budget constraints. Undeterred, we enlisted the help of Bones, another dear friend, to join forces in our quest for the perfect abode. And just like that, our trio set out on an adventure of epic proportions – House for three, please.

After much deliberation, we struck a pact: two years of cohabitation, with an option to reassess should anyone wish to part ways. It seemed like the ideal arrangement, especially considering that both Garthy and Bones were deeply committed to their significant others at the time.

As we settled into our new digs, we wasted no time transforming the space into our personal sanctuary. From installing a colossal projector screen TV, a table-football table in the dining area, and a full-size pool table in the kitchen that Bones and I purchased on a food shopping trip to Costco (with a makeshift piece of wood to place on top for a kitchen table). We converted the garage into Bone's room. A computer room so we could play online Poker against the world, cheating as much as possible, as we could join a table and all see each other's cards – remember, this was before the online games were clever enough to know we were playing from the same IP address. The only thing missing was a sound system.

That job was left to Garthy and me, and I had a pocket full of money as I had recently received the £30,000 payout from my Ireland car accident. As we walked into the 'Bose' store, the sales guy looked at us with a nonchalant glare as if to say, you can't afford anything here.

Despite this, we sat down in their purpose-built 'sound room,' a large 55" TV with the movie Saving Private Ryan playing... a rolling piece of the opening sequence of the gunfire at the Omaha beach D-Day landing. Wow, we could hear the gunshots from 360 degrees around us, bullets shooting past our ears from left to right, right to left. The five-speaker sound system was amazing.

'How much, mate?" we asked,

"£5,000," he replied, with a giggle.

Gulp... Gareth smiled at me and said, "Go on, you know you want it! Imagine how good this would be in our house".

"I'll take it," I said... I think the bloke nearly fell over, and inside, so did I ... £5,000 on some speakers!

Daryl, Me and Gregzy

As the months flew by, our humble abode blossomed into a hub of communal living, where laughter, camaraderie, and the occasional raucous party filled the air. Friends had keys, and there was always something going on. At one point during a fireworks evening, our little 3-bed semi-detached had over 120 people dancing and partying until 6am.

But all good things must end, and as the two-year mark approached, we bid farewell to our beloved bachelor pad. Garthy and Bones embarked on new chapters of their lives with their respective partners. In contrast, I embarked on a journey of self-discovery, embracing the transient nature of rented accommodations and the endless possibilities that lay beyond the horizon.

Chapter 8

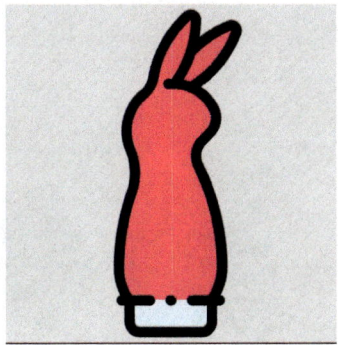

Mischief & Maturity

During my teenage years, I felt like I was part of this older generation of family guys who looked after me. It was a carefree time – I was only fourteen, and my Dad was often away in his caravan. My Mum, well, she was out living her life with Titch, and my life became intertwined with my brothers and their mates. They became my de facto family, the guys who had my back when I needed them most.

One vivid memory stands out: Pops allowed me to ski with twenty-one other adults. I was only fourteen, and Mike was the next youngest person on the trip. Yes, I was the kid in a group of grown-ups, but it was an experience I wouldn't trade for anything. I continued skiing for the next five to six years, becoming quite good at it and absolutely loving every moment on the slopes.

That first year, at the cock-sure age of fourteen, I was allowed to drink half a pint for every whole pint that the adults were downing. I had to participate in all the drinking games, play spoofs, and do everything the others did. The only difference was that I drank halves. It was brilliant, except I was dying to keep up with the grown men, who were going for it each night. I threw up every night of that trip and spent more time with the drunken 'whirlies' than is healthy for a teenage boy.

I vividly recall the trips with Gary, Mike, and the older gang. These guys took me under their wing and treated me like a younger brother. I don't know if I should share some of the wilder tales, but let's just say they really looked out for me. We had an absolute blast.

Brothers: Gary, Mike and Me

On one trip, Gary set himself quite the challenge – he had to include alcohol in every drink he consumed for the entire week. This meant even his morning coffee or orange juice had some booze in it. By the end of the trip, he had gone from being a skilled skier to being unable to tie his own shoelaces – an understandable outcome, I'd say!

Throughout my teenage years, I was lucky enough to go away for three weeks every summer to the Costa Brava in Spain with Dad, Ann, normally Nicola and Paul (Ann's children) and either Matt or Alan. The campsite was terrific, Castel Montgri. It had the largest swimming pool in Europe and was huge. Depending on the different levels on the side of a mountain, it would take you 20 minutes to walk from one side to the other. However, with its five swimming pools, eight bars, and so many sweet and drink huts, you never actually felt you were walking for longer than a minute or two.

Once the caravan was set up and our extra tents pitched next door, we were free to do whatever we wanted for 3 weeks. It was a teenage playground. This was where I 'became a man', so they say, to a 21-year-old girl from Auchtermuchty, Scotland (no idea why I remember this, but not her name). I was 14, and we had been drinking at the bars, but we ended up back at my tent. Can't say I remember much about it, but I'm sure I rocked her world during those three and a half minutes.

I have a hundred stories about my time at this holiday camp. Still, one that stands out was when I decided to take advantage of the Spanish buy-one-get-one-free offer on cocktails. Again, 14 years old and now full of bravado, I decided to join the stage show in front of over 2000 holidaying families – a hypnotist. He had me barking like a dog, laying eggs, wearing X-ray vision glasses. All family-friendly things, unlike another time I chose to be hypnotised for the Ibiza Uncovered TV show; that bastard had me getting naked and touched up by a hot woman. Unfortunately, her husband was watching us from the front row – sorry mate, we were under hypnosis (I think!?!). Anyway, I digress; the holiday camp hypnosis show came to an end just as all the alcohol kicked in. I left the stage, walked directly to the bathroom, and passed out, smashing my face into the sink, splitting my lip and pouring blood everywhere.

Rather than picking me up, the guy who found me thought it would be a better idea to walk to the DJ stand on stage and shout out to all 2000 people: "If anyone knows Mark, the lad who was just laying eggs on stage, please go directly to the toilets where he is passed out drunk." Thanks, mate.

Unfortunately for me, that's not the end of the story. Alan and Nicola came rushing to help me; they dragged me out of the toilets, past everyone, and towards our tent (half a mile away!). I couldn't move, my legs were being dragged behind me, but luckily for them, I had somehow managed to pick up a broad Scottish accent (maybe from my special few hours the night before with 'Miss Acuchtermuchty'). 30 minutes later they laid me down in my tent, and quite rightly went back out on the piss...

A few hours later, my Dad and Ann returned to the site when they saw a man leaning inside my tent. Dad sprang into action, full protection and fighting spirit, only to be told that the man was helping a young lad who had been sick everywhere and was clearly intoxicated. Dad got me up, hosed me down, and ordered me to sleep – I, on the other hand, wanted to tell him my story and how much fun I had been having... all in a broad Scottish accent. He kept telling me to shut up, but all I could respond was, "I cannae dae it" Doh... we were all grounded the following day, as I somehow managed to blame Nicola for 'pouring' the drinks down the throat. Oops, sorry, Nic.

Miss Acuchtermuchty opened the gate, and the following few years were interesting.

The last day of school was enjoyable; I was the chairman of the Committee and school Council and was responsible for giving a speech to all the parents and leavers before a load of us had planned a big night out crawling the pubs of Reading. I remember waiting in the head teacher's office 10 minutes before I was due on stage with a beautiful girl who was my 'deputy chair'. A redhead, wearing a tight red dress, We knew we had a few minutes spare, caught eyes. Before I knew it, I was pushing all the books and folders from his desk onto the floor as we recreated a scene from many a movie, only to hear the footsteps of the deputy head a few minutes later coming closer, a quick straightening of our clothing. I was on stage 2 minutes later, addressing a room of 300 like butter wouldn't melt in my mouth.

Later that night, the drinks flowed, and the buzz was in the air. As the night ended, I became pretty cosy with a particular young lady. With Mum and Titch away for the night, I thought, "Why not invite her over?"

But as we strolled up to my front door, a classic "uh-oh" moment struck. My keys had gone missing in action! No worries, I figured. Our back patio door was always a bit of a rebel. I'd wiggled it open countless times before. Except this time, it decided to play by the rules – double-locked. In my highly inebriated state, I couldn't let this great opportunity go to waste. So, what was my brilliant solution? Grab a garden chair and hurl it right through the kitchen window – smash!

I clambered inside and unlocked the door. The morning after, when I bid farewell to my lady friend, reality hit me like a ton of bricks. I had to be at the car dealership for work in 30 minutes, but my head wasn't having any of it. So, I called the boss and spun a little tale about a break-in and the impending police visit.

Then, in a stroke of sheer brilliance, I actually dialed the police. My reasoning? To keep Mum and Titch from suspecting anything fishy. About an hour later, a couple of officers arrived. I craftily explained how I'd been snug in bed, completely oblivious when the burglars must have smashed the window, spotted the alarm, and bolted.

Unfortunately, I underestimated the police's cunning. They brought in an ace detective who started dusting for fingerprints. "Not the brightest of burglars," he quipped, "left their prints all over the window inside." Lo and behold, there they were, my ten fingerprints, five on each side of the broken window. Blast!

Thankfully, that escapade marked the end of my criminal career, as I've stayed squeaky clean since then. My fingerprints may be on file, but they've stayed far away from any investigations. The real icing on the cake? My buddy Alan found it hilarious and couldn't resist dropping hints to Titch for the next few decades. To this day, I'm still not sure if they ever suspected it was yours truly!

On one skiing adventure with Gary and Mike, Pops (Dad) joined us. I must have been around 17 years old at the time. I was sharing a room with Pops, but for one night out, I left the club with a girl (well, a woman; she was 35, if I remember correctly). Later, while in the room, I heard Pops banging on the door as he wanted to go to bed. I couldn't open it because we were both still in bed. So, we simply pretended we weren't in there. He returned to the nightclub to find out where I was. I quickly dressed, returned to the club a few minutes after him, and acted like I'd been there the whole time.

Conner, Me, Gary, Ben and Mikee

It was a moment that made me realise just how much of an influence my older brothers and their mates were on me. I won that award and continued seeing the girl for a few months after the trip. We still get on via social media, although I haven't seen her in over 20 years.

Chapter 9

Saved by a 'Stranger'

It was November 5, 1997. I was eighteen. Mum and I flew to Belfast for my cousin Hugh's wedding. I've always loved weddings, and we planned to have the best weekend with family we only see on special occasions. Unfortunately, fate had other ideas.

I had left the wedding mid-evening with a girl named Kelly-Ann, whom I had only just met there. She was Hugh's new stepdaughter, and we hit it off pretty fast over the canapes. She mentioned she had a friend with a car, and we all decided to leave the evening party for a little drive We wouldn't be long back before anyone knew we had gone.

It was a cold and crisp winter evening with mist creeping down the hillside, and I was in the rear left seat with my right arm casually draped around Kelly-Ann's shoulders. We were driving through dark and silent country lanes of the Northwest Belfast mountains, and her friend was trying to show off; I didn't think much about it, as I had had a few drinks and was happy to be sat cuddling up close to Kelly-Ann in the back seat. The next thing I remember was being home in England 2 days later.

The idiot driving thought jumping a stop sign at a crossroads junction would be a good idea. He was speeding at over 70mph when a box van smashed into us at full force from the side. Our car flew through the air, flipping multiple times, taking out a telegraph pole and a bunch of hedges, and eventually landing about 250 metres down the road on its roof.

Because my arm was up around Kelly-Ann, my elbow hit the right side of the car with force, taking the brunt of the impact, dislocating my arm bone and pushing it towards the centre of my body, just below my neck and collarbone.

I was knocked unconscious, hanging upside down in the car, bleeding like crazy. The next thing I knew, I was waking up in the hospital for a few seconds before passing out again.

The force of the impact meant that Kelly-Ann had been thrown from the back of the car during the crash. But once the car finally came to a stop, she chose to crawl back in, unplug me, and drag me out of the wreck before the vehicle exploded (she obviously believed the movie scenes!). Kelly-Ann messed up her knees really bad in the process and ended up needing plastic surgery to reconstruct. She physically carried my unconscious self over her shoulder to a nearby country house, where they called the police and an ambulance. She was only a tiny girl, so this must have been all the adrenalin taking over. The couple in the front of the car were injured but okay. We took the biggest hit in the back.

Chapter 10

Crashing the Wedding (Literally)

The wedding party got the news, and everyone raced to the hospital. When you have the Wife's daughter in a car crash, it's a real show-stopper.

I can't say for sure how long I was knocked out, but I've been told it was well over an hour. We all applied injections, tests, X-rays, glueing, stitches, and braces at the hospital. I heard our family took over the whole ward, as we were treated in separate cubicles. You had 30+ drunk Irish family members crying, getting involved where they were not needed and arguing... the doctors didn't know what hit them!

They sent us home separately in the early hours (probably for some peace and quiet), but that turned out to be one of the most painful nights ever. The hospital rang up Mum at 6 in the morning, telling her they'd sent me home without actually putting my dislocated arm back where it belonged.

When we got back to the hospital, we had another pain injection before they sat me sideways on a chair, with the back of a chair in my armpit, and pulled my arm outwards, then down with such force the doctor nearly flew through the closed door, finally relocating it. Eight hours late, mind you.

We were all still alive, and that's what mattered most. But the accident changed my life in a big way, both mentally and physically. I was on medication for 6 months, had to re-sit my final year at 6th form, couldn't play any sport, especially football, for around a year, and even when I got back to it, I couldn't take throw-ins because my arm would pop out, Garthy became an expert at relocating it back in with a snap, to the disgust of every other player on the pitch.

Chapter 11

Crashes and Consequences

I have to question whether a near-death experience counts as life changing. You can't know what comes after, so it's hard to be profound at the time.

There I was, five years later, 23 years old, still having to deal with the mess caused by a reckless driver. He was driving like crazy, showing off, and it ended in a car crash that messed up my body for the rest of my life. I still can't move my arm correctly, can't sleep on it, and have had pains every day since. A reminder of either how close to death I actually came or how lucky I was.

I settled for £30,000, which felt like great money then. But looking back, I realise I should've asked for much more, considering the pain in my shoulder that never leaves. Hindsight and the wish for closure can quickly change your priorities.

Life after the accident was like a bunch of fights – not just with the pain in my shoulder but with all the feelings it brought. A few months later, something small set off a big argument with Dad. It wasn't his fault, but I just lost it. All the emotions I'd kept inside for 18 years burst out simultaneously.

We had been navigating around each other, Dad and I, while engaging in everyday things such as making tea and talking about work, all the while, with the accident a few months earlier still on our minds.

The day it all came spilling out was like a storm. Tea-making was a sacred ritual, so I was trying to concentrate. Dad and I argued about something silly, an offhand comment, and suddenly, I was crying and completely lost it. It was like all the pain and suffering from 18 years just overflowed. The floodgates opened, and I couldn't stop the frustration, anger, and sadness.

I am silent for a moment, readjusting my thoughts. Dad asks, "Is this going to be your life? So closed up about it?"

"Maybe," I say, a touch unsure. I know it's just snatches of an incident—a string of close shaves in one moment. Some moments felt never-ending, and in some, time blurred.

We talked for a while about everything; my childhood, my parents' divorce, growing up, the crash that could've killed me, illness, life, and death.

There will be stories I must cut short or cannot say much about. I don't want to throw anyone under the bus. But suffice it to say, we talked through the evening.

I explained that I didn't fully remember the thought of dying but that I was struggling to control my emotions since the accident and how sometimes I thought it would have been easier if the accident had ended differently. This may have been how I was feeling, or it may have been the emotions of an 18-year-old who's just been told he has lost a year of his life and needs to stay at school.

Confused and worried, Dad tried to figure out why I broke down. But at that moment, it wasn't about the argument or whatever started it. It was about everything – the car crash, the pain, the heavy stuff on my shoulders, both in my body and my feelings.

Dad explained to me that there was no greater fear than the worry of losing a child.

We stood there, trying to make sense of the mess. Dad tried to help, but it was hard for us to understand what happened. It was a natural and vulnerable moment, a crack in the tough front I put up to handle the problems I faced every day.

I started to get sensory flashbacks of the crash; the smell of oil, the darkness, the heat, the sound of the engine, the shattered glass... and the silence from the aftermath of a late-night country crash, just screaming.

That breakdown changed things, a significant release of all the feelings I kept inside for almost two decades. It made me face not just the pain in my shoulder but the hurt the accident left on my feelings. The lawsuit, the money, none of it could make the constant ache or the hidden scars go away.

Looking back, that moment with Dad showed me the truth I was avoiding – that dealing with the car accident wasn't just about justice and money. It was about figuring out a life changed by pain in my body and my heart from a broken home, fighting every week since I was a toddler, and finding a way to carry that weight without letting it take over everything.

Chapter 12

A Journey Through Memories & Healing

I struggled to settle in the aftermath of the accident, the restlessness and discomfort lingering, unable to escape the burning sensation that the spotty memories brought.

Despite attempts to move forward and suppress the pain, the fear of a similar incident recurring became a persistent barrier, preventing any genuine progress and leading to feelings of suffocation and an ongoing imaginary fight within my mind.

The house and my current lifestyle felt increasingly confining, pushing me toward an overwhelming urge to run away from my problems. Whispers in my head incessantly urged me to seek help, the weight of unresolved issues intensifying.

Fortunately, Gary's friend mentioned Roger Hepburn, a therapist whose assistance became a real lifesaver, not just once, but twice in my life. I don't believe in guardian angels, but if I did, Roger was mine. My emotions ran wild and felt like a clamp squeezing tightly against my head as I drove to his house, a small bungalow over the other side of Reading, and he welcomed me into his living room. There was a piano and two chairs, one of which looked far more comfortable than the other. He instructed me to sit in that one.

With his calming demeanour, Roger suggested a unique approach – closing my eyes, taking a deep breath, and delving into the part of the mind that doesn't actively think but retains memories and allows for expression. Although it sounded peculiar, this method proved surprisingly helpful. He entered my subliminal mind via hypnosis & NLP (Neuro-linguistic programming). He openly talked about the mind and memories you have locked away, pulling out feelings and memories. My mind spoke back openly.

Roger listened empathetically as I shared painful memories, offering support without judgment. The experience in his presence brought a profound sense of relief and safety, solidifying the therapeutic bond that was becoming increasingly valuable in my journey toward healing.

The car crash might have started it all, but those sessions with Roger became a journey where everything from my childhood started pouring out. It was tough, really, and tiring, but it also turned out to be the best thing that could have happened to me. I didn't even know I was carrying this enormous weight that had been lifted off my shoulders.

Every week, as I sat in that chair, relaxed and just talking, Roger guided me, well, without me even realising it, down the memory lane of my home street. Door number 1, "What colour is it? What does it look like? What could I see when I open the door?" Door number 2, the same questions, and so on. I realised that only a few years gave me problems, while most of my childhood was happy. But door number five was black! Even I knew that meant something important – the year Mum left.

With Roger's help, I started to see the complexity of my history. Some doors opened to a flood of happy memories, while others hid things I hadn't considered. It was like a journey to discover more about myself, and with each session, I uncovered layers I didn't even know existed.

The hypnotic trance allowed me to explore my thoughts and feelings, digging into why I felt scared and worried. It certainly wasn't just about the car accident; it was about figuring out my past, understanding its different parts, and facing the tough stuff behind door number five.

With his calming voice and helpful techniques, Roger became a guide through this maze of memories. The process was strange, but it helped me deal with and make peace with the hidden parts of my mind.

All I knew was that after every session, I had to sit in my car for around 10 minutes composing myself, and when I got home, I was shattered... I went to bed after every session for an hour before I was ready to get back into the real world. Only to wake up with a transparent and weightless feeling that I could think clearly, and the pressure inside my head was gone. After a time, I was back to my optimistic self, but this time, it was different; I felt better, more robust, and had a clear vision and drive that was missing before. I knew who I was again.

If you take nothing else from this book, please remember the following:

IF YOU EVER FEEL LOST, LONELY, OR THAT YOU DON'T KNOW WHICH WAY TO GO, PLEASE TRY THERAPY – IT MIGHT JUST SAVE YOUR LIFE

Chapter 13

Instincts and Opportunities

D oing well in business often comes down to trusting your instincts and following your feelings. It's like having a built-in compass that helps you make good choices while navigating the sometimes-tricky world of starting and running a business.

You must be good at determining which new opportunities suit you and whether a job is a good fit. Sometimes, you have to grit your teeth and push through anyway to support yourself. It's about finding the right balance between dreaming big and being realistic, making sure you pick paths that match what you're good at and want to achieve.

It's like making big life choices, like finding a new home or starting a family. It's about connecting with yourself, trusting yourself, and choosing paths that align with your most important values and dreams.

After going through some tough times, both in sports and education (I failed my Business Studies course as I really wasn't in a good place for learning after my car accident), I left school in the rearview mirror and jumped into the working world. I was apprehensive but ready to face whatever challenges and opportunities awaited me. Thankfully, this is when everything seemed to fall into place and became far easier for me... I loved working.

When I was 18, I got my first real job with ONDigital, which later became ITV Digital. They were about bringing digital TV to people's homes through the TV antenna. Out with the old analogue systems, in with the new.) I was part of a team of about twenty-five people, and my job was to teach electronics stores about this new digital TV revolution.

Even though I was the youngest in the team, I excelled quickly. My personality and determination made me stand out. Although I made many mistakes, I remember booking a meeting with a manager of the electrical store Currys in Newport once. I knew Newport from my time at the caravan in Southsea with Pops (as it was only a short hovercraft ride), which I watched hundreds of times as I walked up and down the promenade between the arcades. I chose to take the car, so I travelled around the coast a little further to the car ferry. One hour later, I pulled into Newport High Street.

After 20 minutes of searching, I just couldn't find the store anywhere, so I called the manager, "Hi, it's Mark from ITV Digital; I can't seem to find you; I'm standing outside the bakers and the bookstore; where do I go from here". The silence was deafening, as he finally responded, "We don't have a bookstore OR bakers on our high street, we are right in the middle, the biggest shop, you can't miss us!!" I was confused, to say the least, what was going on? How? And then, as I heard the twang of his accent, the penny dropped... "Err", I stumbled my words out. "Are you in Newport, WALES?? "Sure am, boy, please don't tell me you are on the Isle of Weight??" Bugger... what a dick!

I had a few minor mishaps along the way, but the customers and my colleagues loved me, so the senior bosses noticed what I could do before I knew it. And suddenly, I led a big team of 500 sales agents who went door to door. This quick rise showed that trusting your instincts and working hard matter in business.

For about six to nine months, I bounced between the bustling cities of London, Birmingham, and Manchester. It wasn't a vacation, though—I lived in hotels from Monday to Friday, navigating each city's unique rhythm as a charismatic and outwardly confident teenager.

During that time, I became a host of countless classroom training sessions for hundreds of people. I was teaching others how to sell, even though I had no training myself; my instincts and natural ability helped me through. As it turned out, I had a talent for it, and the whole experience was a blast. I spent each day teaching others how to be a successful door-to-door salesman and every evening out knocking on the doors, finding out what the hell I was supposed to be doing!

Living a hotel life taught me some valuable lessons. One of the quirky challenges was figuring out when to avoid knocking on doors. It was a bad idea in London during "EastEnders," and in Manchester, interrupting "Coronation Street" was a definite no-no. People take their TV shows seriously, and getting in the way can make them seriously ticked off.

I remember knocking doors, only for people to open their upstairs windows and shout at me. I always smiled a cheeky grin and asked, "If I knock your windows, will you please answer the door?" Making people feel at ease may have been my teenage superpower.

Despite the challenges of constantly being on the move and learning the intricacies of TV schedules, my first job was nothing short of phenomenal. It shaped me and gave me a taste of the real working world.

After my fulfilling time at ONDigital, I felt the itch to try something different. The world was full of opportunities, and I was ready to explore. So, I began the exciting journey of searching for new horizons and fresh challenges.

Chapter 14

Navigating the Digital Highway

I found myself in a new role at Whirlpool washing machines as an area manager, again looking after retail stores and wholesalers from a head office in Croydon, but this time with budgets and targets to hit. I loved it and quickly landed some of the largest and most secure deals in the country. My friendly demeanour, helped by the fact that Pops, Gary and Mikee were all doing the same role (albeit in far more senior positions) in their own companies, Pops in Petrol with Jet, Gary in kitchenware with Prestige, and Mikee with a new company every six months. From sweets to chewing gum, medical to stationary – he always had itchy feet, looking for his next move.

After nine-twelve months, I took a sharp turn into a new career path: Auto-Trader Online. It was a significant change, and little did I know, it would open doors to a competitive industry with promising pay.

In this new realm, I quickly found my footing. The industry was fiercely competitive, and my colleagues were all striving to climb the ranks. Despite the challenges, the allure of the potential rewards kept me motivated to carve out my niche.

I quickly spotted an opportunity and seized it. I took on the role of National Accounts Manager, a position that showcased the importance of the skills I was developing in the industry. It was a moment that affirmed my capability to thrive in a position usually held by people double my age.

The switch to Auto-Trader brought its own set of challenges. Unlike my previous role, where face-to-face interactions were the norm, a significant part of my work now happened through online exchanges or telephone calls. Despite the adjustment, I saw this as my new arena and determined to make it work.

I dealt with senior staff within the international car brands, Mercedes, Porsche, Ford, and Kia, to name a few. However, it was Kia that gave me my big break. I managed to sign the biggest deal the business had ever done and couldn't believe the commission I was being paid.

In this digital landscape, the art of negotiation is a crucial skill. Whether through written exchanges or spoken words over the phone, I took every opportunity to hone my skills for navigating deals and agreements, taking every piece of advice people gave me.

Despite having many innovative ideas and bringing concepts ahead of their time, my job wasn't a smooth sail. It came with its challenges, primarily stemming from the misplaced distrust some had in technology and car dealerships, or perhaps both. The journey was marked by an intense grind I had to keep hitting head on.

What kept me pushing forward was the promising prospects of success. The allure of commission played a significant role in fuelling my determination.

Despite the initial scepticism and challenges, I embraced technology as a tool for success. Learning how to leverage it became crucial in navigating the intricacies of the job. Adapting to technological advancements was not just a necessity but a key to staying ahead in the game.

If I didn't know what I was doing, I would learn it. Attitude is Everything.

Chapter 15

The Birth of Richie Winter

"*S*omeone's got to do it," a phrase I have spoken thousands of times over the last 20 years. Literally! I can't remember the first time I said it, but after working in the industry, I was about to start working in, it just rolled off my tongue time after time. It's like asking a taxi driver, "What time do you get off?" Or "Busy day?" I could hear it coming out, but I had no control over stopping it...

At 22, I asked myself, "Should things change?" Time to go up, sideways, work in a more prominent place, or be more independent?

After pondering this question for a while, I went for a few beers with my brother Gary, and we spoke about possible avenues of careers and new opportunities. I asked his advice and whether he thought I should take a risk at this time in my life.

After a long pause, Gary said, "Well, I've had this idea and been working on it recently..." He then tossed out a wild card—a new business idea named Richie Winter Ltd.

"Richie Winter Ltd?" I echoed, intrigued. The name alone sparked my curiosity. Gary went on to unveil his vision, and it was bold: an enterprise selling adult toys online and through intimate women's home parties. It was a daring idea that aimed to challenge norms.

Richie, short for Richard...Winter, the opposite of Summer—he wanted to create a new Ann Summers business! I loved it, and not just because he was my brother.

His vision was audacious: an enterprise dedicated to selling adult toys online and through intimate women's home parties. It was a daring proposition that promised to challenge norms and redefine boundaries. I wasn't expecting the usual business idea, but Gary's excitement was infectious. The more he spoke, the more I was drawn into the uncharted territory of adult toy retail. Some might describe it as bold and slightly seedy, but those opinions didn't bother me. It actually felt natural to me.

I grappled with the idea of entering a world outside traditional business norms. The more Gary explained, the more I saw the potential for breaking barriers and challenging societal taboos. I was intrigued by the idea of being part of something that could reshape perceptions.

I agreed to join in. I wanted to know more and be a part of this.

Gary's proposal wasn't just a concept; it was an invitation for me to take on the role of Sales Director. A single 22-year-old hungry for the unexplored, I found myself at the edge of an unconventional venture. The idea of being at the forefront of this bold endeavour excited me. The journey ahead was uncertain, but the thrill of breaking new ground overshadowed any reservations I might have had.

As Gary and I got into the details of our business, we focused on the practical stuff. Things like how to sell, how to make people interested, and where to get money were all important parts of our plan. Gary didn't let the fact that our business was a bit different stop him—he decided to go for it.

Gary took charge, and I stood by him, ready to face the challenges of selling adult toys. The journey seemed exciting and uncertain, but I was committed to supporting our vision every step of the way.

Starting Richie Winter Ltd. had its challenges. We knew that some people didn't like the idea of adult toys, Banks wouldn't take us on, Accountants refused, but we were determined to challenge and change those views. The whispers of what people thought couldn't stop us as we tried to change how people saw adult products.

Against what people thought was normal, Richie Winter Ltd. showed that we were okay with doing things differently. We didn't know it then, but the road ahead would have both tough times and good moments, but it would certainly give us some fantastic life stories.

Chapter 16

Transformations in Business

Working for Richie Winter Ltd and its distribution arm, RW Distribution (and then finally, Wingpow International, our Manufacturing business) during those initial years was an exhilarating adventure. Beyond the boldness and ingenuity that defined the enterprise, our unbridled passion truly set us apart. While we may not have been amassing fortunes like some industry counterparts, the sheer enjoyment we derived from our work fuelled our journey. The adult toy business, it seemed, was on an upward trajectory, and we were right in the midst of the excitement.

Embracing the single life, I navigated a whirlwind of experiences while jet-setting across the globe. The odd, this-way-that-way lifestyle became my norm, characterised by consumer trade shows and weekends that were wild and exhausting. It was a life that defied expectations, filled with everything you could imagine and more.

In the realm of dating, my life took on a thrilling pace. Award-winning movie stars, Playboy models, and even personalities from live adult TV channels became part of my social landscape. After-show parties became a heady mix of passion, allure, and a touch of excess. Between the ages of 22 and 25, every moment was soaked in the excitement of business parties that had to stay trade secrets. If anyone knew what was happening at these events, it would have caused a media storm. Thankfully, I was right in the middle of everything, perfect age, perfect attitude.

Flights and random meetings became a riot of conversations, whether I was travelling solo or with friends. The moment I revealed my profession — selling adult toys for a living — it wasn't just their interest that was piqued. It didn't matter if they were with their partners or if our acquaintance was a mere five minutes old; the allure of the adult toy business captivated minds and sparked intriguing discussions. Ladies would open up in seconds and tell me all their fantasies; some went far further than that. When I thought I was good before, I was superhuman now. Although, many of these stories are for another day.

Having spent considerable time fantasising about such experiences, I found myself dreaming and actively living the dream. There was a palpable shift, a turning point where the line between fantasy and reality blurred. Something about this lifestyle flipped a switch within me, transforming my experiences and confidence.

As the unconventional journey unfolded, my confidence blossomed. Our chosen profession's unique experiences, intriguing conversations, and sheer audacity contributed to a newfound self-assuredness. The oddball path I had chosen was not just a job but a catalyst for personal growth and self-discovery. Little did I know that these early years at Richie Winter Ltd would shape my professional trajectory and redefine my understanding of life's myriad possibilities.

Apart from the parties, we also made a huge business impact globally. We were the first business globally to take naked female photos from adult toy packaging, the first brand to change the names from Dong or Dildo to descriptive words like Heaven and Passion, and we were the first brand globally to stop using the horrible standard flesh colours of white, mocha and black, changing them to bright pinks, purples, yellows etc. Gary, Adam (Gary's best friend & our business partner,) and I were getting an industry name for ourselves. Worldwide, we were disruptors and innovators, and I'm proud to say I was driving many of the creative changes and ideas.

Chapter 17

Jokes, Jigs , and Tales of Mistrust

I 've got a truckload of stories from those times, but I don't know where to spill them all. There was that time I got invited to the live recordings of adult TV programs because I was seeing a couple of the girls on camera. The night after, I was back home with a bunch of mates, and those same girls started talking about me on live TV. One of my buddies, who was in another house, got all confused and rang the TV set to ask if they were actually talking about me. I, Garthy and Bones sat in the house we shared and heard the whole conversation on live TV. Ten minutes later, he showed up at our house, laughing his socks off and giving me a round of applause!

The Erotica shows in London, Manchester, and Edinburgh were a blast. They were a place for anyone with an interest in sex to attend. We called Fridays "Freaky Fridays" as it was a great excuse for anyone with a real fetish to take a day off, come down and get changed into whatever they feel comfortable in. It was fantastic, and I want to point out that we never thought they were freaks – just people who liked certain things different to "the norm." There were people dressed in all leather, all rubber, being walked on dog leads, in cages, cross-dressing, transgender, every ethnic and sexual persuasion possible, and it was amazing, as everyone was welcome, nobody judged, and it was all in the theme of having fun.

We sold our toys to the enthusiastic public, had drinks with the customers on our stand, had our own little secret store cupboard, and partied all night with "John the high-end Banker," dressed in only leather chaps, or Susan, an accountant by day and dungeon master by night. We made tens of thousands in sales over the weekend, and it was the kind of job where you'd forget it was work.

Gary and Me enjoying Wingpow success. Brand and Design award at Las Vegas CES trade show

Gary and I were known as the "English Brothers," with Adam thrown in the mix. We got along with everyone, shared drinks, had great laughs, and were always in the bar, taking the mickey out of anyone we could. We knew about 95% of the people in the global adult industry, and they all knew us. Anyone not in the industry wanted to be with us—we were in the cool club!

One day, we found ourselves in a large open bar in Berlin, filled with 250+ industry people who were busy talking shop, relaxing, and enjoying themselves after a busy trade show. Gary and I chatted with a few industry pals at the bar when I became restless. The same old stories were being rehashed, and I felt like stirring the pot.

I decided to get up and do a lap around the bar and tables, announcing to everyone that Gary was about to showcase his Irish dancing skills. I may have talked to about 20 tables of people before returning to Gary at the high bar stools. When there was a break in the conversation, I took my chance to change the subject, talking up Gary's dancing prowess, saying he was an Irish Dancing champion back in 1995. Gary played along, confirming that he was a champion, though he had to quit due to a knee injury.

I took the opportunity to ramp things up even further, with Gary none the wiser about my overall goal. "Come on, Gary," I said, "give us a little jig. You know you can still do it. Come on, Gary. Dance... Dance... Dance... DANCE..." I got louder and stood on my stool, rallying the people surrounding us to join. "DANCE, DANCE, DANCE." Soon, all 250 people in the room chanted with us, shouting, "DANCE, DANCE, DANCE."

Gary, with a cheeky grin, turned to me and muttered, "You fucker." He had two options: laugh it off and retreat or actually get up and dance. Gary tells this part of the story perfectly because he says that for one brief second, with all the chanting, he thought he could pull it off. So, he stood up, stepped into the large open circle that had formed around him, and jumped... only to land awkwardly, clutching his knee.

"Ah," he said, "sorry, everyone. My knee can't do it."

I led the massive cheers, and we all returned to our drinks.

To this day, he's never really forgiven me.

Chapter 18

Navigating Industry Dynamics

S hortly after a wild day, we were all mixing it up at the after-show party. One of the salesgirls from a trade magazine approached me, and we hit it off to a substantial extent. She was someone who could take the job in stride, and so we laughed and drank through the night.

It was easy to stay partying into the early hours. The energy in this industry and at these celebrations was almost always positive.

When it was time for bed, she took it upon herself to walk with me to the lift.

"It's late. But I'm not so tired. Maybe I could come to your room?" she asked.

I smiled and politely declined the invitation. To be honest, I was tired and just wanted to sleep.

The following day, I came down for breakfast and saw the girl from the night before talking emotionally to one of the guys on the industry circuit. She pointed me out, and he stood up and angrily charged me.

"What kind of cunt are you?"

The tone in which he fired insults and dirty names at me was baffling. Telling me that I should *keep my private parts in check*. He told me that I needed to go and apologise to the girl. I was confused and taken aback.

What I didn't know was that he had walked past her after I left her the night before, and she was crying. He jumped to conclusions, and the assumption was that I had slept with her and then kicked her out.

When these rumours started the morning after the night before, I ended up being the recipient of confused and suspicious glances. Everyone was talking about how this guy, Dale, had yelled at me in public.

I decided to keep quiet. I didn't want to embarrass her and didn't care what others thought of me. But I also didn't want to call her a liar or make her feel awkward. I could handle a few sideways looks and a bit of gossip.

Thankfully, she was a great girl. She came over after hearing about the incident and apologised immediately. She said she was just drunk and disappointed I said no. She didn't say anything else. That evening, she explained everything to the big group, and Dale was so embarrassed. We all had a good laugh about it, and everyone kept saying, "What's wrong with you, Mark? Why didn't you take her home?" It was all in good fun, and we laughed together. I was grinning on the inside as I pride myself on being respectful to women; I loved the chase, but if they said no, it was always enough for me.

I knew that everyone in the industry saw me as a decent guy.

Chapter 19

Don't Leave Your Keys Lying Around

The office's humdrum routine continued, and it seemed like just another regular weekday morning. Gary, Adam, and I were going about our business, awaiting something to break the monotony.

In need of a break, Adam proposed a lunch run, and I agreed without much thought. My Vauxhall Vectra 2.0 might not have been the most stylish car, but it served its purpose. Little did I know that this lunch break would turn into an unexpected twist.

The decision to buy a Vauxhall Vectra for nearly £3,000 was prompted by an unfortunate incident involving a milkshake thrown at me from a passing school bus a few weeks earlier. Even if it wasn't the coolest choice, a new car was necessary.

There I was, cruising in my Nissan 100 with the top down, feeling the breeze, when a rogue milkshake from a school bus turned my smooth ride into a disaster. Drenched in dairy, with my car's insides looking like a modern art piece, it was clear – my days of flaunting that soft top were over. No amount of scrubbing could erase the memory or the stains. So, with a chuckle and a sigh, I bid farewell to the Nissan. Sometimes, showing off just shakes up trouble!

Adam was gone from our office that day with my Vectra for quite some time, but apart from being hungry, I didn't think much of it. That is until four 'weeks' later when Adam approached my desk, chuckling to himself as he placed a VHS video tape on the surface.

Adam's lunchtime escapade didn't seem extraordinary at first, but things took an unexpected turn four weeks later. He was chuckling to himself.

The shock set in as I saw the front cover of the video— a naked woman with one of our products on the bonnet of MY car. My number plate was unmistakably visible, and the video was shot right in the farm warehouse unit where we stored our products. What a wanker.

Curiosity got the better of us, and we played the tape. To our astonishment, it was one of our friend Matt Bath's productions under the banner of "Asphyxiation movies." The scenes featured two or three girls and a handful of men engaging in 'fun' activities in my car—front, back, on the steering wheel, even my poor gear stick, and more.

I had been driving that car for the last four weeks unknowingly. Only one thing to do, sell my poor Vectra. I drove it straight to the scrap yard, and was offered £12.20, a fraction of its original value, "Deal," I said, another poor car relegated to the scrapyard with memories I'd rather forget.

Chapter 20

Innovating the Toy Industry

In 2003, the adult toy industry was evolving for the better. Previously, the UK and Europe had these seedy sex video shops selling rather unsavoury, flesh-coloured toys made from unpleasant materials. But we decided it was time for a change, a revolution.

As I mentioned, our ideas were simple yet ground-breaking: removing the explicit imagery from our packaging and introducing bright colours. And with that, the European TopCat Brand was born. We were pioneers in transforming the adult toy industry on a global scale. Over the next two decades, I personally became the most awarded product designer in the industry, creating the world's top-selling products and collaborating with major brands from both adult and mainstream industries (although the secret, behind-the-scenes winner, as I always designed for our customers' brands).

Initially, we started with in-home parties where women invited their friends over for a Richie Winter Party (like an Ann Summers party, but with a Richie twist). Gary, Adam, or I would guide the ladies through our products, giving them some space to enjoy drinks, and then we'd return to answer their questions and make some sales. Some of these parties got pretty wild quickly! But what we realised was that most women faced the same issues when it came to their sex lives. They worried about similar things, and their husbands and boyfriends had identical behaviours. We quickly became experts in understanding women's needs, desires, and concerns.

Our business grew through wholesaling to adult shops and selling directly online. In stores, we created a branded wall with all our products neatly packaged and looking like a legitimate brand instead of a mismatched collection of unattractive toys with dodgy names. We struck a deal online with a budding retail company called Amazon, where we became their site's exclusive adult toy brand. Unfortunately, about a year later, we had to ask them to remove their 'Marketplace' sales (people who listed their own products on the site) because they were selling toys too, which was against our agreement. Amazon told us they couldn't turn off 'Marketplace,' so we had no choice but to discontinue selling toys altogether! Haha, if only we could have foreseen the future!

We started the toy manufacturing business with Budiman Lee, the Chinese/US condom sales brand owner who sourced the products from Chinese factories. In early 2003, Lee approached us after one of our biggest potential customers launched a toy collection that was an exact copy of our products. Lee wanted to build a factory but couldn't gain people's trust, so he asked if we would join him as business partners and be the company's face while he handled the Chinese side of the operation.

Dinner in China with our management team: Gordon, Sam, Cherelle, Lina, Crystal, Nicholas, Budiman Lee, Me, Local Council, Head of Coca-Cola for China, Zhang, Wendy, Wang, Dong, Simon and Dong.

It turned out to be a perfect match. He invested $2.5 million in the land, and the first building was constructed in 2004. Over the next 18 years, we built the factory together, with 100% of orders coming into us in the UK and the factory management overseen by Lee. We achieved sales of $20,000,000+ a year through our UK business, employed over 350 staff in China, built a sizable 12-bedroom house, and spent approximately two to three months in China working with our talented team, with whom I became great friends. It was an incredible journey working in China. I felt blessed.

My role changed from Sales Director to Company Director over the years, overseeing the company's global strategy and operations. One lesson I've learned is that you should approach everything with the best possible attitude. As I've told Danni a thousand times, "Attitude is Everything."

Mum, Roger, Danni and Me, at our house in China

Gary is the creative force in our partnership, with the ability to create brands and write compelling copy. In contrast, I discovered I have a talent for product design and engineering. Together, we made a fantastic team. Over the years, I became an unofficial engineer for the business, designing new and unique products that shaped the entire toy industry globally.

After working closely with Gary for two decades, we developed an uncanny understanding of each other's thoughts and actions. We knew how to work seamlessly together in front of customers, and we had a telepathic ability to know when to talk, when to be silent, and when to collaborate to help our customers.

Chapter 21

Revolutionising Pleasure

My appreciation of the industry was clear-cut.

Our days belonged to whatever was new and exciting – the innovation. Nights were for celebrating the things we had made and the successes we achieved. Days off were not strictly a thing in our line of work. We wanted more, so we worked more.

We loved the work that we did.

Once I start work on a project, I don't tend to stop and don't slow down unless I absolutely have to. But in the world of the adult toy industry, things could get unusual. It's an arena that can grab your attention, pulling you into a life that might seem weird to many. The things people find alluring—stuff that's secret, not normal, or a bit out there—have a way of making you want to explore places you've never been.

With flashy displays and colourful outlooks, the business has this odd charm. It promised an escape from regular 9-to-5 humdrum and offered variety. It was a mix of adult make-believe and real-life desires taking the spotlight.

As I was sucked into this differing world, there were times when I felt like I might lose myself. The adult toy scene has special groups with their own talk, trends, and communities. It's easy to get caught up in it, where what's not normal becomes the usual.

Gary and Me working in Russia

Even with all the exciting opportunities around, I always made sure to keep myself. It was important to remember what mattered to me and who I was, especially with the revolution happening before my eyes.

Did you know that sex toys have a long and surprising history, reaching back over 28,000 years? Our ancestors got creative with materials like stone, bronze, camel dung, and even bread. Yep, bread! The idea might sound a bit odd, but it turns out the desire for pleasure has been around for a very long time. The market for these intimate products has thrived since the days of Rome.

Gary, Adam, and I wanted to create adult products that stood out and had staying power. We aimed to design items that would be visible on the back shelves. We dreamt of products that mainstream pharmacies, maybe even big names like Boots, would be proud to carry and sell in the future.

We were determined to be different in a market that often stuck to the same old formula. Innovation became our guiding principle as we set out to break the mould in an industry that was ready for a change. We were prepared to challenge the norms and redefine what adult products could be.

"People want to be secretly blown away. They like a juicy secret. That's true of everyone," we thought.

I can still vividly recall our consumer shows. We'd chat casually with women about what they wanted and how they intended to use the products. It was all in good fun. We'd throw out some silly questions, and they'd fire back with equally ridiculous answers. Then, after a quick chat, they'd choose a product in a matter of minutes but take a whole ten minutes to decide on the colour.

We'd ask all sorts of crazy questions, like, "What colour are your curtains? What's the hue of your bedspread?" Anything to get them giggling and enjoying themselves.

Gary and Me during Covid-19 Lockdown in Bermuda

The funny thing is, the colours didn't really matter in the end, but they were important to them, you know? So, we went with it and made it a memorable and nonjudgmental experience.

Our goal was simple—to sell products and make the whole experience enjoyable and light-hearted. We wanted our customers to have fun while choosing and remember the experience with a smile. And you know what? It worked. Our unique approach started to turn heads in an industry known for its more serious and explicit nature. We were ready to keep pushing boundaries and adding a splash of colour to the world of adult toys.

Chapter 22

Fifty Shades of Opportunity

People aren't just attracted to what you're selling, especially not in our day. It's also heavily based on *how* you're selling. They want to see a story behind your brand, something that will make them curious, pull them in and keep them coming back. This happens, I believe, when people recognise a certain desire in others. Their clothes, their behaviours, their surroundings, their talk. It's easier to do that if you carve out your own path.

I, Gary and our business partner Adam had created a niche for ourselves in the adult industry. Trudging from place to place like anyone and everyone, rocking a casual look, just wouldn't cut it. We wanted to treat our ambition and our business like a proper one.

So, what would make us stand out?

Suit up.

We stayed smart, pressed shirts and ties and suit jackets.

And it proved to be the right move.

We treated our business like a treasure. The years spent building it from the ground up became extraordinary, and it just kept growing.

A multimillion-dollar company.

But I wasn't about to forget what had brought me here.

We also had an amazing mix of personalities. As we found out, the whole industry wanted to work with us. No matter who we were selling to—individuals, small shops, or large global organisations—one of us fit precisely what the customer was looking for. So, we played the game. In specific meetings, it was Gary and me; in others, it was Adam and Gary. We understood what would work, so we made sure it happened.

In 2011, the world went wild for the new book Fifty Shades of Grey. It was a game-changer for the toy industry. Suddenly, everyone wanted to buy toys, and it became a global phenomenon.

On this particular day, I was contacted by a lady who owned the licensing rights to the book, and she wanted to launch a new toy collection using the brand and the book's name.

We met at a trade show in Birmingham and had everything set up to design and manufacture the toys for the "'50 Shades of Grey" brand. There was just one hiccup. We weren't an established retail website. I understood they were after a quick win, so I had no real option but to pass them on to two friends who owned a small but growing online store called Lovehoney. Neal and Richard were over the moon and got to work immediately.

In 2012, Fifty Shades of Grey toys were launched. Lovehoney went from being a roughly £10,000,000 turnover business to a £60,000,000 global powerhouse retailer, selling more toys than 95% of the retailers worldwide. We made some toys for them and did alright, too, but their success was on another level. Ouch—first Amazon, now this.

Chapter 23

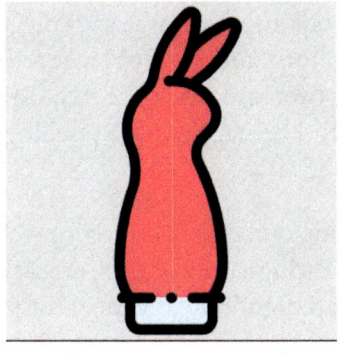

Oops

A couple more stories from my time working in the industry always make me chuckle, so it would be rude not to share them here, too.

One involves a new product we purchased from Australia as exclusive European distributors. It was a set of two personal shavers. These were the first of their kind, long before all the leading brands started selling intimate area shaving systems.

The products were excellent and worked really well. One cut personal hair into the shape you wanted, and the other product "buffered", making it smooth.

We sold loads of them and even offered free demos at trade shows, which was interesting... We flew the product owner over from Melbourne for a trade show, set up a seat, and offered women to sit down, and he would shave their private parts – it was all a little weird, and I stayed well away, but he loved it, and so did the willing participants. Unfortunately, the show organisers didn't have the same sense of acceptance, and after four hours, they came over to kick the poor guy out. We tried everything to reason with them, but no, he was removed to have a holiday in London.

After the show, I called him to congratulate him on the product's success and explained that there was only one issue that I needed to change if we were to continue selling the items... I wanted the photo of the strange-looking hairy man he had used on the box changed to a woman. The call went silent for a minute before he explained to me that that hairy Australian bloke I was talking about was actually his wife!! I nearly died... I think I dropped the phone and, point-blank, refused to pick it back up. Thankfully, Gary took over and saved the day, explaining that I was only joking and that we would be happy to keep selling the product exactly as they were. Ouch...

Another thing that made our time working so well was that we could fly around the world for meetings, trade shows, or just nights out. I have flown a few times to Vegas for a night out, always in business Class, as the airline staff knew and loved us.

One night out in Hong Kong with a customer, we went for a lovely sushi dinner, followed by beers, and ended up in a nightclub, drinking tequila until 5 in the morning. As I stumbled back into my hotel lobby right in the middle of Wanchai, a busy district both day and through the night, I smiled at the staff as I entered the lift and went to bed minutes later... only to need a wee. I remember opening the door to the toilet, and it was closing behind me; that's strange, I thought. Then I opened my eyes. I was in the corridor, naked. Fuck. As I crept out of the lift and over to the hotel reception covering my modesty with my hands but displaying my arse to the hundreds of office workers now walking past the huge glass windows to the road, I sheepishly asked for a key to my room, only for the girl on reception to smile, and every so politely ask me for some ID.

I thought that was the end of the story until I finally woke a few hours later, late for my flight and needing to get my backside to the airport in record time.

I made the plane, just the last person on board, still pissed and smelling of last night's antics, for the air steward to smile as she passed me a glass of champagne. Phew, I made it with only my dignity damaged until I pulled out a receipt for over $1,000 for tequila. Double fuck. What a night.

I remember once having to fly to the US for a meeting, It was near a great mate of mine, Neil's house. So, I landed and drove down to him for a day before driving up to New York for my meeting. You may have seen the movies of New York or tried to drive there yourself, but it's a complex task. I soon realised that I was lost and would only make my meeting if I took drastic action. I saw a sign saying, "Parking $10." I pulled into a tiny area with 2 cars parked up. It wasn't a car park, and it had nobody official looking working there, but I had no choice. A guy in a tracksuit and hoodie came over, "$10 bucks," he said... I paid, gave him the rental car keys, and started running to the main road to find a taxi.

The typical yellow New York taxi pulled up, and I hurriedly got in; as we pulled away, I realised that I had no idea where I was and would have no way of ever finding the car again... "Stop the cab," I shouted. He pulled over, and as I jumped out, leaving my laptop bag in the back seat, I rushed into a hotel nearby, picked up one of their business cards from the counter, and ran back to the car... problem solved! I hoped.

I managed to find the car after a successful meeting and beer with our new client, and the feeling of relief was enormous. Sometimes, you must take risks to get the rewards... although I could also imagine my phone call back to Gary in the UK explaining that I lost a Hertz car rental somewhere in New York.

Chapter 24

Patents and Pioneering Ideas

My twenty years in the adult toy industry was more than a job; it was a chance to change a whole industry and bring it into the mainstream. I didn't just work in this field; As I mentioned, I led the way in creating some of the world's best-selling and most innovative adult toy products.

Even though I wasn't trained in electronics or engineering, I had a natural talent for designing new products. My ideas and designs weren't just about making money; they were about being creative and using new technology—driving the industry forward.

This approach led to unique products that were patented worldwide. These products were not only popular but also won many awards. One of our most significant achievements was when one of our products won the "Best Personal Health Product 2019" award, beating well-known products like "Fitbit" at the world's largest consumer electronics show, CES, in Las Vegas.

This win was memorable. It showed that our products were more than just adult toys; they were part of health and wellness. Our hard work improved lifestyles and challenged old ideas about what our industry could do.

Looking back at these 20 years, I was driven by my endless curiosity and love for making new things. It was a time of constant innovation, changing how people saw our industry. Those years weren't just about building my career but about leaving a mark in a constantly evolving field.

For those who are interested, I thought it would be good to list a few of my original ideas over the years and the products that we patented and sold globally to the world's largest retail businesses and brands.

Patented Touch Sensors:

- Idea creation: Inspiration from a chance encounter during a "product design day"

- A woman detailed how she stopped using products when her young son walked in, and she couldn't turn the product off. She became embarrassed and never touched a toy again.

- I designed a product with internal sensors that only turned it on when it came into contact with the skin. To turn it off, you simply let go.

A few years later, I developed this design further, so the deeper the toy went, the more powerful the vibrations. We created additional features for the sensors, and Touch Sensor was born.

Patented Throbbing (Heart Throb):

- Idea creation: Envisioned a toy that mimics an accurate pulse of a penis.

- this still remains Ann Summers's biggest-selling rabbit to this day, with over 200,000 pcs sold in 1 year.

Patented Sequential Motors (Multi-Motors):

- Idea creation: Rather than making a product actually "thrust" up and down, I wanted to create the feeling of a product actually moving up and down, so I hid several motors inside the product and wrote different functions, ensuring the motors turned on and off in specific sequences, giving the feeling the product was moving.

Patented External Motors (Freedom):

- Idea creation: I wanted to "free the motor" from the standard internal shaft of a product, so I got a sock and a tennis ball and started to twirl the sock until the ball was encased. Holding the sock's top and bottom, I could see exactly how I wanted the motor to vibrate freely and shake from side to side. This became a big motor inside a thin, flexible silicone sleeve, and the Freedom motor came to life.

Body Resonating Motor Tech (Water Splashing):

- *Idea creation*: 2004 at Reading Festival, slightly inebriated and buzzing from the legal magic mushrooms they were selling, I was listening to The White Stripes on the main stage, and they played their song Seven Nation Army. Wow! My breath was taken away from the baseline pounding through my body. I wanted to vibrate a toy through the body like this, so I started researching how?

What does music have/do that would improve our standard vibrating motors? I realised that if we could make a vibration that resonated with water, our bodies would be 80% water. If we could lower the frequency of our vibrations, we could spread the vibration throughout the body, hitting far more nerve endings and deeper than anyone before.

After a year of trial and error, we cracked it with our engineering experts in China. A vibration that actually resonated with your body – just like the sound resonates in a car when you are driving fast and open the window slightly, that disruption of air banging into each other making the low-pitched "Whar, Whar, Whar" sound that hurts your eardrums.

Our body-resonating tech has become a staple in millions of products globally.

"IP" LED Light Tech:

- Idea creation: After having our extension in our home, I realised that all home renovation now included LED lights – so why not on our product, too. Give people a cool disco as they are having fun. I wanted to hide the LEDs under the silicone to turn on at just the right moments and also to the beat of any music playing or the beat of the vibration setting.

'IP' Turbo:

- Idea creation: Adding a "TURBO" button to a product sounded like a right giggle. At the right moment, the user could press "TURBO", and a second, hidden motor, placed at a different angle, would automatically turn on for between 15 and 20 seconds. Giving the user the biggest power rush ever.

As you can see, I had some fun creating these new products... although I sometimes wish even more that I could be a product tester.

Chapter 25

Love and Beer at The Spring Inn

Let me share a story from the Autumn of 2004 at the Spring Inn. This place has always been like a second home—a cosy country pub with wooden floors and a fantastic vibe.

I'd been drinking in them after work for some time and took out a couple of the waitresses, but one day, I had no idea what had changed. Suddenly, I started flirting with the bar manager named Ruth. She's a lively redhead, cocky, with stunning eyes and a personality that's just full of life.

I've always had a thing for redheads, but Ruth was on another level. She wasn't just the person behind the bar; she was like the heart of the whole place. Feisty? That's putting it mildly. People couldn't help but be attracted to her lively energy at the oak counter.

Ruth and Me

She was honest, with no pretences or hidden motives. Ruth was straight up, charming, and didn't put up with nonsense. She put me in my place a few times and could handle herself with any punters. From that day forward, the Spring Inn had a new energy to its familiar surroundings.

I feel bad that I didn't know or care much about the girls who had been behind that bar before, but with Ruth, I wanted to know more.

At first, she gave me the cold shoulder, you know? They say something about meanness and keenness, but it didn't bother me. It actually made me more determined to get to know her. Something was interesting about finding out what was beneath that frosty but fun surface.

Our conversations went from passing by and ordering drinks to real moments where we connected. Whether it was chatting while she poured or sharing laughs at a joke, those talks became the best part of my visits to the Spring Inn. Ruth had this way of making someone feel at home as if the pub were her own living room. But I wanted more...

After a few months, things changed between us. She finally gave in and accepted picking me up from town after I had a night out with the lads.

It felt like a whirlwind romance, but I was totally into it. The timing felt right, and we were having a great time together. We went on mini-breaks and spent as much time as we could with each other. She would drive back to mine every night after work, and it quickly became serious.

Our relationship grew from those unsure moments at the bar to something more profound. Ruth and I weren't just enjoying each other's company at the pub; we were exploring life together. Was this the moment I had been waiting for—no more one-night stands or meaningless relationships? I had a few very serious relationships in the past, but I was a teenager and not ready to settle down, so this felt completely different. Was she the girl to stop me from wanting to be with anyone else?

I won't ever forget the day Ruth – or as I call her, Rosie (she ate like the big girl from the girl Shallow Hal, a 90's movie, but looked like the sexy thin girl, - Gwyneth Paltrow who was called Rosie.) Anyway, Rosie called me at work after a few weeks of dating.

She was in my bed mid-morning and sounded concerned after her late shift, whispering, "Someone's coming up the stairs." I lived with Garth and Bones, but they were at work, so I didn't know who it was. Then I heard a voice I knew ever-so-well. My Mum introduced herself, "Oh, hello, my name's Pauline. "Nice to meet you.". I can still picture Rosie just pushing her arm away from her naked body under the covers, to shake my Mums hand. Oops... She hasn't forgiven me for that yet!

Rosie and I got serious quickly, and we knew it was the real deal. The pub where we used to talk business became where our love story began.

As time passed, our relationship changed with the seasons. We were inseparable, facing the good times and the challenging moments that come with building a life together. We were spontaneous, good, and happy.

We *are* happy.

Chapter 26

Time to Grow up

When Rosie came into my life, it was like a big change. Suddenly, all the wild parties and flashy adult toy stuff didn't seem as cool as just hanging out with her.

Before Rosie, my life was all about excitement and adventure with random strangers. The adult toy industry, with its glitz and glamour, had its thrills, but something was missing. I always knew that I was a family man inside, but I either wasn't at the right time of my life or hadn't met the right girl. This time, I did, and it made me happy, although Gary and Adam couldn't resist teasing me.

Together with Ruth's parents. Roger, Linda, Ruth, Danni and Me.

They claimed I had "lost my mojo." I understood what they meant, but I didn't mind. I had changed purposefully and by choice.

Rosie brought a calm and a feeling of belonging that I didn't know I needed. Our nights turned from loud parties to quiet talks, movies and shared laughter. Knowing someone was waiting at home became more comforting than the crazy lifestyle I used to have.

Very quickly, the idea of starting a family felt right. Having our own little family made life more exciting and meaningful. The wild parties and crazy adventures of the past started to feel like far-off memories, not as appealing as the simple joy of being with Rosie.

She became the most essential part of my life, and the thought of becoming parents together made us feel happy and purposeful.

Although we didn't live together properly, I realised the real richness of life wasn't in big parties or the flashy industry I used to be part of. It was in everyday moments, like watching her take a shower! Haha. (not everything changed.)

Chapter 27

Journey to Parenthood

I was at football on a Sunday lunchtime when Rosie called me. "Can you come into Boots to see me before going to the pub?" This was where she worked, so I knew something big was about to happen. "I'm pregnant", she told me, then punched me and swore a few times. I was ecstatic, and went straight to the pub with my mates to celebrate!

Ruth hates surprises and is impatient, so as soon as she arrived at work that morning, she spoke with her closest friend Chris, walked over, picked up a test off the shelf, and went to the bathroom.

Becoming parents got us all excited and very nervous. Rosie and I were in for this adventure together. We were thrilled about having a little one, but we also felt nervous about the responsibilities coming our way.

We stuck together, side by side, the whole time. Rosie's pregnancy brought its own set of challenges, but we faced them as a team. Dealing with body changes, soreness, and emotional ups and downs, we took each step hand in hand. We had to quickly buy a house together and move in... nothing like doing things efficiently and in order.

Rosie's strength amazed me. I got a fundamental understanding of what women go through during pregnancy. She handled fears, ups and downs, and all the challenging parts with a swear word and a smile.

We found comfort in the simple things. Cooking meals at home turned into a particular bonding time. Instead of big, noisy parties, we preferred quiet talks. It was a small change, but it meant a lot. We embraced the simpler joys of life, looking forward to the journey of parenthood. We figured out that real happiness comes from those intimate moments shared between two people getting ready to welcome a new life.

I had some worries about myself. Would I be good enough? Could I be the father I always wanted to be? Was this really happening to me? To us? But I quickly gained control of my thoughts and remembered what a gift this was. Parenthood came with uncertainties and self-doubt, but as I navigated these concerns, I began to see that the journey itself was a precious gift. Worries transformed into opportunities for growth and learning, and I embraced the profound responsibility that awaited.

I would love to say that we had tranquil, quiet moments before our family expanded, where we cherished the beauty of this transformative journey. But no, we were in panic mode, moving into a new house. I was still working, and we had to decorate the house. We still needed real money at this stage, but the business was certainly looking up. We had to borrow £25,000 from Ruth's parents (Roger and Linda) to afford the mortgage, but they were happy to get rid of Ruth once and for all! ;-)

Chapter 28

Welcoming Danni – A New Chapter

Life changed in the blink of an eye the day Danni, my little lady, came into the world.

Ruth woke in the middle of the night and started pacing, hanging out from our upstairs windows before waking me It's time!

It felt like time had stopped as I tried to understand the news. Then, it hit me—let's do this!!

The maternity ward was buzzing with new life, and we were ushered into a room before being told to go away as it was too early. Come back in a couple of hours! What... what are we supposed to do now? We drove around; I filled the car with petrol, which pleased Ruth, asking Ruth's Mum if she wanted anything from the shop, and then we went to meet her dad, who was off to play golf.

When we returned to the hospital, it was all systems go.

Unfortunately, Danni was twisted, so the Midwife called for an emergency C-Section. I was thrown my surgery outfit and told to go into the bathroom to change.

Only to come back out with nothing on my bottom half. They had given me two pairs of tops, and I'm not sure if it was on purpose, as the nurses and midwife found it far too amusing to have been their first time trying this!

Straight into the theatre, it felt like 20+ doctors appeared, one of them pushing my wheelie chair straight to the back of the room, far out of the way. She said in a very matter-of-fact, doctor-speak, "I'm the Baby doctor." But my brain wasn't working, so I replied, "You don't look like a baby to me." It didn't go down as I expected, and they all turned and started working on Ruth.

It was the most frightening experience of my life. Emotional, scared belief, and as the father, utterly and completely helpless. You are only in the room because people tell you that you need to be. I'm sure the doctors would much prefer it if the father was sat in the waiting room as they used to do a hundred years ago. Nevertheless, I was allowed to stay and kept a very close eye on the top half, speaking to Rosie throughout, although I'm sure it all fell on deaf ears.

A few minutes later, I heard, "Come and meet your daughter," from the tiny Midwife looking at me holding a tiny crying bundle. I took hold of her, bent down to Ruth, and as we were asked, "What's her name" I looked at Ruth, and I said, "How about Danni?" We had discussed a few names, but she looked like a Danni. Rosie agreed, and I felt like I grew six inches taller at that moment. Anyone who has been through childbirth will understand when I say you look at your partner in a new way afterwards. You are in awe of them and what they just did, and you are immensely proud, as it's undoubtedly the most amazing thing ever.

Looking at Danni, my new little girl, it felt like time slowed down. Everything around us seemed to calm, and I remember taking a deep breath, soaking in the moment. The hospital machines beeped softly in the background. But in that room, it was like a bubble, just Danni, Rosie, and me, held together by pure adrenaline.

Chapter 29

Becoming a Father

After the whirlwind of emotions at the hospital, I needed a moment to process the fact that I was officially a dad. All "Dads" were kicked out of the hospital at 9 pm sharp. 20:00, and I was already looking at my watch. I had the most amazing experience in my life. Still, I really wanted to slip out to my family and friends to celebrate with a beer, something I fully accept that only the dad can do in this situation, but what better way to celebrate than a pint at my local The Fox & Hounds to wet the baby's head. The jungle drums went out, and I had time for a quick shower before raising a glass or two at the pub.

Walking into a familiar atmosphere, I was greeted with cheers and hugs from the regulars who had become a part of our journey. More importantly, I want to thank my brothers and closest few friends. This pub often felt like a second home, largely down to the memories, and it was only fitting to celebrate this milestone here. Pints were raised, and everyone took the piss, letting me know that my life was now officially over as we toasted and downed whisky. It was a moment I'll never forget, especially now, as not everyone is here anymore.

The following day, fuelled by anticipation, I rose at the crack of dawn with a banging head, eager to return to the hospital. I was unable to go in right away as it was 6 am, so I decided to make a quick pitstop at Tesco. I was in the middle of the shop, surrounded by an array of pink baby items, filling my cart with all the essentials. Standing in line to pay, a man in a business suit, probably on his way to some important meeting, couldn't resist asking, "New baby, is it?" My emotions, usually tucked away in public, exploded. Tears welled up, and I blurted out, "She's mine! Her name is Danni! I'm going to see her now!" The arrival of Danni had transformed me from a stoic figure to a blubbering mess at the mere mention of her name.

Going back to the ward felt different. The crazy excitement from last night was replaced by the bright morning sun, but the amazing reality of being a dad stayed with me.

Nothing in the whole wide world could compare to that special connection we had in that instant. It was like this magical feeling, a mix of love, being responsible, and realising how amazing life is. Holding Danni, I knew this was just the start of a whole bunch of incredible moments, and I couldn't wait to be there. I was finally ready to be a dad.

Life took a swift turn for Rosie, juggling her career and newfound motherhood while adjusting to the whirlwind of changes. From a single lady to being in a serious relationship and suddenly becoming a mum – it was a lot for her to handle.

Dad & Daughter

Within a year or two, her world had morphed into something entirely different from the free single girl she was just before she met me. The challenges stacked up, especially with Rosie unable to drive post-C-section, but I did everything I could to help. I was lucky to own a business and took a few months off to help at home. I still worked, just from home; it made it easier for us all. In my eyes, Rosie was nothing short of incredible; she had done her part, and now it was my job to help.

Our life was far from the conventional "normal" but extraordinary. Danni showed me how important life was, not just in business but in the little everyday things that often pass us by.

One of my favourite stories with Ruth came a year after Danni was born. Ruth wanted new and improved boobs, and who was I to deny her such a luxury (She's actually had two new sets now, what a shame! Haha).

I dropped her off at the hospital near Harley Street in London and knew I had to waste a few hours while she was getting prepared and in surgery.

I was excited to see what her new perfectly formed and sized breasts would be like, so I thought, I know, I'll go for a pint.

I found a local old-fashioned London pub nearby and ordered a pint of Guinness. A few minutes later, a TV star from Eastenders (one of Ruth's favourite shows), a character called Minty, walked in. I was about to sign the card I had just brought for Ruth, so I took the opportunity to have one of her most loved actors sign it, too. I approached him and politely asked, "Excuse me, my wife is in the hospital down the road, and she loves you. Would you please sign her card?" He looked up and then at the card I was holding out in front of him, and he replied, "Oh, congratulations, of course I can".

It was at this moment that I realised that the card I was holding had a picture of two babies' bald heads and the saying 'Congratulations on the Twins" (I thought it was funny!). I smiled a smile; only a man whose wife was in getting her boobs enlarged could smile as I explained that the babies were, in fact, only for me. He burst out laughing and asked me to sit down with him. Three more pints of Guinness later, I stumbled back to the hospital, over an hour late, and tried to explain to a very frustrated and very medicated Ruth what had just happened and why I was now pissed. Fair to say, she didn't believe me and wasn't very pleased!

Chapter 30

Blue Bloods, Bonding Over Football

Despite the constant ribbing I get from my mates, I've always been a Bluenose, a proud Everton supporter. I secretly love the fact that there aren't many of us—we blue bloods are a rare breed, and I wear that badge with pride. My love for Everton dates back to when I was just a young lad, around four or five years old.

My Dad, or Pops as I called him after my own Pops (Dad's dad), wasn't really into football and didn't support any team. My brothers, Gary and Mike, were both Man Utd fans, but I was determined to carve my own path from a young age. The Anderson family, who lived opposite us, were huge Evertonians. Gordon, the dad, and his son Ian, a few years older than me, were ardent supporters. I vividly remember Gordon taking me to my first game in Southampton. We won, and that's all it took – I was hooked!

Right from the start, I loved Everton, so I loved a challenge. It was always going to be a volatile mix of ups and downs. We were never one of the "top, high-flying clubs," but we didn't need to be. Not with the best supporters in the world.

These were the good days. Liverpool was the more glamorous and successful of the Mersey teams, and elsewhere, teams like Arsenal and Manchester

United were running the show. I wasn't the only Everton heart beating around, but it felt like it to me sometimes.

I don't know how you're meant to react to supporting a team that doesn't always come up trumps with trophies, league victories and the like. But it set a fire in me to always want to go that extra mile, see myself winning, and focus. It's a feeling that's never stopped.

Danni was an Everton baby right from the start. I remember she was only a few weeks old when she became the first Everton kid. She had Everton pillows, a duvet, and everything Everton-related you could imagine. She slept with all that blue and pink Everton gear.

Everton forever together

Speaking of pink, Everton even had some pink stuff by then, which was pretty cool, as it matched some of the other clothes Rosie picked out for her to wear, meaning I could sneak in an Everton top without her realising! She was my Everton sidekick, and I couldn't have been prouder, as it brought us together in so many ways. From sitting watching our team on TV (before she even knew what football was), she would sit with me, drinking from her bottle and looking up at me with trust and love in her eyes... come to think of it, I'm not actually sure I watched any of the football either.

When she became a toddler, we would both bounce around the living room anytime Everton scored – again, she probably had no real reason why, but we were doing it together, and that is all that matters between a dad and his daughter.

For over eight seasons, the ritual of travelling to Liverpool and watching Everton with Danni has been a highlight of my life. Our travels to the stadium were never just about football; they were adventures. When Danni was little, she'd giggle like an innocent seven-year-old, urging me to make up goofy lyrics for every song on the radio. Those three hours on the road flew by in a blur of laughter and off-key tunes.

As Danni grew, so did our journey traditions. Our car rides turned into singalongs, our voices perfectly synced with our favourite songs (mainly 90's R&B, Usher, Blackstreet, Destiny's Child, Babyface, etc.,) although she taught me about new music, keeping me "cool". It was a special bond, the kind that's rare and precious. When we opted for the train, we'd play cards and laugh over games, the clack of the tracks a steady backdrop to our fun. Those trips meant just as much as the matches—maybe even more, considering Everton's shaky form since 2010.

We made the most of our trips, regardless of the match outcomes. Staying in hotels became a mini-vacation, complete with swims and shopping sprees. But it was the mornings we cherished most—sitting down to the "'best-fried breakfast ever," as Danni would say. Those meals were a treat, a perfect start to our day, no matter how the game ended. These weren't just match days; they were our days—filled with the simple, joyous moments stitching life's fabric.

I realised I was in a position to do something impossible for me, so in the summer of 2017, I put Danni forward to become a mascot at Goodison. Like most things, money talked, and after paying an additional supplement, we had fast-tracked the process. As the day arrived, we woke nice and early in our hotel room in Liverpool city centre, went for our obligatory fry-up, and made our way to the stadium. The sun was shining bright, a perfect day for football. Danni had five hours before kick-off in the Pre-season match against Seville. The club had set up everything to ensure all the kids were looked after thoroughly. They all received a kit, training staff, a tour of the stadium, football training with the parents, and a penalty shootout competition before they were taken to the pitch side to meet all the players and have photos taken. It may have been because Danni was the only girl, but they sat her right next to the players for some reason. My hero and one of England's best-ever players, Wayne Rooney, sat shoulder to shoulder with my daughter – I was shocked and a little jealous!!

I was taken to my seat with all the other parents and told to wait for the kids to walk out with the players onto our hallowed turf – somewhere I had always dreamed of stepping but never had the chance. Danni and the others were allowed on the pitch to warm up, kick some balls and wait for five minutes before kick-off for the players to arrive.

They were taken back down the tunnel to be matched with their player, and as the traditional sounds of the sirens of Z-Cars started to play throughout the stadium, and a packed crowd got to their feet and started to cheer, I could see our leader, our Captain, Phil Jagielka, lead the team out, with Danni holding his hand. Wow... she wasn't only a mascot. She was leading Everton onto the pitch.

They completed the lineup and were told to run off the pitch and find their seats with us, the parents.

I captured a photo of Danni running off the pitch. The look on her face is pure magic, joy, and shock all in one. It's a moment that will stay with me forever, and hopefully, something Danni can look back on in years to come and remember—I sat next to Rooney!!

Chapter 31

Adventures Together

As she grew, I wanted to show her the world. I can't remember exactly when our first trip together was, but she was only three or four months old. I just took her everywhere with me.

Rosie wasn't too fond of flying, and she used to fly with me on a few holidays before Danni was born. But she soon decided that was enough and hasn't flown since. I've tried many times to get her away with us, but as I mentioned, she is stubborn, and once her mind is made up, that's it. I wish I had chosen not to travel by boat or train; that would have been far better for us all.

Travelling the World Together

So, it was Danni and me, travelling the world. We went to Spain to visit Pops and Nanny Ann, visited Turkey several times, and even went to Lapland to see Father Christmas. Our first step off the plane was a shock, as the temperature was a bone-chilling minus 20 degrees. We went to a place called Levi in Finland, and it was like a bit of skiing and sledging village with only four hours of daylight each day, but our hotel had 17 pools, so we were good no matter what time it was.

I remember dinner time on the first evening at the hotel; they'd set us up at a table. I had Danni with me; five other mums were there with their kids. Danni was the only young girl there, probably six or seven years old, and I was the only dad without a partner. We were seated at a singles' table, which I found a little unusual, but oh well, I started talking to all the single mums, and it turned out they were all divorced and living a single life with their children.

Travelling the World Together

I decided to make things interesting and told them that I, too, was a single parent, that my wife had passed away, and I was taking care of my daughter all on my own. Well, that did the trick – they all swooned and offered to help however they could. I could see Danni was shocked, so I gave her a wink. She would give me those eyes that said, "Why did you say that?" She asked me why I'd made up that story as we left the restaurant.

But it was all in good fun and gave us a good laugh.

I should probably apologise to Rosie; it may not have been the best thing to say, but it was hilarious at the time.

Our adventures continued the following morning when we met Father Christmas, experienced thrilling husky rides, and had an absolute blast. But during that trip, I'm pretty sure she saved my life – you see, I've saved hers about five times, but she had her turn to save me once and thankfully took it.

It was a freezing night, about minus 22 degrees. We decided to go for a midnight walk. The town was quite a distance away, and we were outside in the middle of nowhere. I dragged her along on a sledge because she didn't feel like walking – lazy cow! As I was dragging, I thought, "This is amazing! The snow is so deep, and it's beautiful." But then she jumped off the sledge, and the trodden path disappeared into deep snow. I decided to follow suit but just disappeared to my armpits as I stepped onto the snow. My whole body was submerged, and it was pitch black around 12:30 am. We were all alone, except for a streetlamp in the distance.

I was stuck, and it was freezing. I couldn't pull myself out of there, and I panicked. I thought about telling Danni to run back to get help, but instead, she crawled back and laid her body down so I could climb outward. It allowed me to get out of that snowy pit. It took about 20 minutes or half an hour, and even though we were laughing inside, I was shaken and wondering if I had taken it too far this time.

Then there were our trips to China. I took her with me to visit my factory, and we saw the whole team there. Granny (my Mum) and Roger came along, and it turned into a bit of a role reversal, the two of us taking care of the two grandparents. We had an absolute scream, eating Chinese delicacies and enjoying ourselves in the amazing pools in Macau.

We travelled to New York in the winter of February 2020 and Los Angeles and Las Vegas in 2022, where we met with a customer of mine who owned the largest Dunkin Donuts franchise in the US. We went for a drink with his family and enquired about our dinner plans that evening. He was having none of it when I suggested that we would wing it at a burger joint. "Come with me, I can sort something for you." So, we got into his car and drove to The Bellagio Hotel. He dropped it right out front, and we walked through the hotel to their famous restaurant on the lake, looking out to the Strip. "These are my good friends; I would like you to look after them as my own family. And charge the bill to me". Wow, I was speechless, as I know it's impossible to get a reservation at this place without weeks' notice, and even then, you are inside. Not for us; the manager physically moved tables outside to make space for our new table overlooking the lake and the world-famous fountains. The food was unbelievable. I will never forget the desserts for as long as I live.

Travelling the World Together - Macau

We also visited Jean-George restaurant, a Michelin-starred steakhouse. There, we ate 3 ounces of A5-certified Kobe Beef at $200 an ounce. This is one of only a few places in the US that serves it. Wow, it was like eating steak-flavoured butter. We each had a side order of filet mignon, too, just to wash it down!

I have a hundred stories and a thousand memories from all our holidays together, enough to write another book. But that's for another day!

When Danni was just a child, she'd gaze up with those big, expectant eyes, implicitly trusting me to fill every minute of our holidays with amusement.

Those early years were a whirlwind of spontaneous fun; I was the maestro of our entertainment, and she was my eager audience. For example, during our trip to Disney World when Danni was nine. As we entered the vast and mesmerising theme park, she looked up at me and asked, "Can I run now?". "Of course, let's go." With that, we ran in big circles, not caring what anybody else was thinking. She was a child at Disney World – what else should she do!

But adolescence brought a shift. Her questioning glance, "What now, Dad?" stopped as she grew into her teens. She knew what she wanted, and I didn't have to be the child anymore. Thankfully, enter Craig and his girls, martial arts enthusiasts like Danni. Their companionship during holidays became our new adventure. Trips with them weren't just trips but escapades of pure enjoyment. From Canada to local jaunts, where ice cream and card games weren't just activities—they were chapters in our shared story of joy and easy camaraderie, precisely what our evolving family dynamic needed.

I needed Craig, him, and me, and the girls became like sisters. It was perfect and at the ideal time. It was a massive help for both of us, and the girls got on perfectly.

Since then, we holidayed (apart from 2022 due to my legal battle). We've been to Canada and saw Niagara Falls and Spain several times. We've always gotten a lovely house with a beautiful pool, and we just chilled. We were on holiday; we went from ice cream parlour to ice cream parlour, went out for dinner and played cards every night together. We just had an absolute scream. The girls loved that, every bit of it, and to be fair, it was precisely what we would need at that time.

My friends often tell me I'm the luckiest and best dad they know. I think they mean it because of my incredible relationship with Danni, which has been perfect from day one. She's the funniest person I know, my absolute best mate, and has brought much joy into our lives. Even now, at seventeen, she is still a source of endless fun, and I couldn't be prouder.

Chapter 32

Unexpected Detours and Travel Adventures

S uccess in business often boils down to trusting your gut. It's like looking at your business and yourself, weighing the pros and cons, and determining if you're both in the right spot. It's almost like a gut feeling—kind of animalistic at times—choosing the path or risk that gives you the best shot. Now, I'm not perfect—I've made many mistakes. But some of those risks? They've taken me farther than I could've ever imagined.

My work used to take me to Las Vegas several times a year for trade shows and meetings, and I have to admit, I relished every trip. The glitz, the lights, and the atmosphere were intoxicating—like a different world—and I loved every bit of it.

Holiday Buddies, Megan, Danni, Clive, Lewis, Sam, Kayleigh, Craig and Me

But one year, my Vegas adventure took a sharp left turn. It was mid-March, and I started hearing rumblings about a volcanic eruption in Iceland, spewing ash into the sky that grounded all airplanes passing through northern Europe.

You couldn't even see the ash cloud from the UK, but they said it was there. And bam, next thing you know, flights between the UK and the United States were on lockdown.

Initially, I thought, "No worries, I have more British Airways flying club membership miles than most pilots – if anyone can find a way onto a plane, it's me." Or so I thought. After a couple of days of persistent dialling, I finally managed to get through to British Airways, and they broke the news that the earliest flight I could catch from Las Vegas would be a daunting two to three weeks away. Wow, I had to think on my feet.

I'll admit, it took the wind out of my sails a bit.

Plans are going down the drain, and I'm stuck in Vegas.

So, I devised a plan – I would fly to LA, work in the office for a few days, and have a better shot at getting a flight out since there were multiple airports in the area. But life had other plans, and two to three days later, they told me it could now be three to four weeks before I could get on a flight home. This was rapidly turning into an enormous problem.

While I wasn't one of the unfortunate souls who needed medication or was in dire straits, I was separated from Danni and Ruth. Danni was just a 3/4-year-old bundle of curiosity at the time and couldn't grasp the situation.

So, I decided to move again. The East Coast of the US boasted plenty of airports, and I could bunk in with Neil and Jo Holloway in Ocean City, New Jersey, for a few weeks until I figured out a way back home.

They are two of my closest friends, and I've grown up with Neil since we were five years old (He was the friend who told me my Mum was on TV!) They both came from Reading and were teenage sweethearts. Neil went to University in the US, studying football at 16, and never came home - Jo followed him as soon as she was 18, and they married out there as True Americans. Anyway, they were absolute lifesavers, welcoming me with open arms. We had a fantastic time together, and I became part of their family while pulling out all the stops to find a way home. They even made a name sign for my room to piss off her sister from back home, who had bagsied it whenever she wanted to stay!

I was so desperate to get home to my family that I considered chartering a boat or boarding a cruise ship. But I wasn't the only one stuck—half the world was facing similar woes.

People had hired rental cars in mainland Europe, driven them home, and then dumped them, causing rental businesses logistical nightmares to return the vehicles to the right countries.

While I was stuck across the ocean from my family, my brother Gary was living it up in a 5-star hotel in Turkey with his family, making the most of his unexpected extra vacation!

I couldn't help but feel a twinge of envy as I was treated to a few snapshots of his picturesque family escapades. I sighed, reminding myself that my situation was temporary. Soon enough, I'd be back home and down the Fox for a pint with mates.

After two long weeks, Neil heard about a local TV news crew looking to interview stranded folks, and he arranged for me to be interviewed. I spoke about how lovely Ocean City was and how excellent Neil was for taking me in (He appreciated the plug).

A news crew member approached us less than five minutes after the interview. "We just got a call from Mr. Donald Trump. He invites you to dinner tonight to celebrate your birthday at Trump Towers in Atlantic City." Crazy, right? We rushed home, dressed up, and went to his resort.

Trump? The Donald? That name echoed in my head as we hurriedly prepared for what was sure to be an unimaginable evening. The irony of being stuck away from home transformed into a once-in-a-lifetime opportunity: Dinner at Trump Towers. I could hardly believe it. Excitement and disbelief mingled as we made our way to Atlantic City's grandeur.

The evening was beyond anything I had imagined. The extravagance extended beyond the dinner table; the management team was at our beck and call, ensuring our every need was met. Yet, as grateful as I was for the unexpected hospitality, the reality of being stranded persisted. A private plane home was missing from the cards.

Another week passed, and the ash cloud began to lift, allowing planes to take to the skies again. However, my only options were to wait another two weeks for an open seat on a flight or pay a hefty £4,500 for a first-class ticket home from Boston. I didn't think twice.

I just wanted to get back to my family. It was a wild few weeks that I'll never forget, and a nice reclining seat at home.

If you've travelled as much as I have, you will understand that getting stuck at airports is something you must accept. I've also flown from London to Hong Kong and into China, flown out to Taiwan for a 30-minute meeting, back to Hong Kong, and home to London, all within 36 hours. I was dead for a few days on my return... but needs must.

Gary and I have also managed to squeeze in a few "holidays"' during our business trips, too, like the four-day trip to Thailand for a two-hour meeting or Bermuda and Antigua during COVID for "Meetings," only to be caught by Danni and Rosie when I stupidly uploaded a photo of me on a jet-ski in the middle of the Bermuda triangle! Oops.

One trip in 2020 was to our friend's (and customer's) ski lodge in the Colorado Rocky Mountains near Aspen at a beautiful small resort called Crested Butte. Gary and I flew into Denver and hired a car to drive to the resort. Unfortunately, the weather had other plans. One hour into our mountain road journey, the snowstorm got so bad that we saw cars sliding past us and deserted on the side of the road. It was like a scene from a movie. We had no option but to crawl back down to the main town and stay the night, choosing to fly out instead the following morning to the small airport at the resort in one of the small US internal planes. We had a great couple of days in "meetings" and eating edibles for the first time (wow, they have some kick) before it was time for us to fly out.

We arrived at the small airport as another storm was closing in. The lady unlocked the padlock for the airport gates, walked us through the small terminal, and then proceeded to check us in. Our flight wasn't for another two to three hours, so we were doing alright until she walked over and told the waiting handful that our plane was cancelled.

The only plane out for the next three days was leaving in ten minutes, and only one seat was available. Fuck. After a quick game of rock-paper-scissors and Big Brother rules, Gary was off to take the last seat.

I was ditched and had no idea what to do or where I was. The airport worker told me I would have to leave as she was locking up, but she could drive me 20 minutes down the road to a bar. It was my only option.

As I sat there with a beer, looking through the internet at all my options, I resigned myself to booking a hotel and staying in the town for a few days. Then she walked back in, covered in snow and wrapped up. "Get your bag. I may have a minibus for you at the airport. You can drive it to the nearest airport that still has planes flying."

What a lifesaver! When we got to the airport, another six people were hoping to get on the cancelled plane with us. She explained to everyone that I would now drive us all "through a huge snowstorm, in a country I don't live in" to an airport two hours away. I have no idea why she chose me to drive, and I know I had no insurance, etc., but we all hurried into the van. I somehow got fleeced for $100 for petrol, and off I set.

By the time we arrived at the second airport, the plane was waiting for us, the pilot was having a coffee, and we simply walked through and straight onto the plane. An hour later, we were at Denver airport, and although I had missed the flight back to London, I was only one step away and could get a flight the following day. This was another fantastic adventure that seems unreal even as I type this. I know I have another 10 more, though... again, for another book or beer at the pub.

It's not just the delays that can cause a scare while travelling to other countries. I've seen killer snakes outside my room in Australia, eaten turtles, bees, and every insect known to man in China, rats as big as dogs in Hong Kong, and lady-boys from Thailand. But nothing prepared me for what I experienced while visiting the US to watch a friend run in the New York Marathon. It was around February 2008. Alan and I flew over to watch Weeman run the marathon, as I was able to arrange a meeting in the city simultaneously. Unfortunately, the day before the event, Weeman pulled a muscle, so it just turned into a weekend piss-up. And what a night we had. Weeman disclosed something personal to us that we promised not to tell anyone. So, I've waited a long time to tell this story, but it deserves to be told. Ever since he was a man, Weeman always knelt in front of the toilet when he went for a wee!?! I mean, every time. One knee up, and one knee on the ground, at home, at his parents' house, stranger's houses... brilliant! We ripped him mercilessly for the entire evening, but he said we should try it. So off I marched to the bathroom in this packed-out US bar, pulled up on crap US larger, ready to give it a go. Walked into the bathroom, straight into the first cubical, and knelt down... I was clearly intoxicated, as no average human would kneel down inside a busy bar toilet, but there I was, taking a lifetime and laughing out as I comprehended how stupid it was. But then, the door swung open, and I was now in full public view of the entire bar. Everyone started cheering, laughing and clapping. I did the only honourable thing possible, I put my hands high above my head, celebrating as my wee started spraying everywhere. I'm not sure the bar owner was happy, but we all had a good giggle.

That was actually a side story, sorry... but I couldn't leave it out.

The problem started when I returned to the hotel in the early hours. A plush place on 5th Avenue, with Alan and Weeman. I got into the nice, clean white bed, longing for a few hours of sleep. "Ouch," I felt a sharp pain in my leg, near my knee. I must have rolled on a hard piece of dust or something, so I pushed the thought to one side and tried to fall asleep. I'm unsure if it was five minutes or one hour later, but my leg started hurting so much that I had to get out of bed to look. My right knee was the size of my thigh, bright red and throbbing with pain. Fuck.

After waking the guys, I phoned the hotel doctor, who came up immediately and suggested it was a spider bite. She could see the two small holes.

I was due to fly home that evening, and I didn't know that seeing an actual doctor or hospital in the US would be a pain. An ambulance to come and collect me costs over $4,000, and although I had insurance, I still never believed they would help.

I checked Virgin Atlantic's schedule for earlier flights back and went directly to the airport. I walked up to the counter and told them I had an emergency and had to fly home immediately. Thankfully, being at the top of their membership scheme, I was offered an economy seat.

Unfortunately, my swelling was so bad that I couldn't bend my leg by this time. I had cut my jeans open to allow my leg to fit, and I explained to the staff what had happened and that I needed to get back to the UK to rest. Suddenly, a wheelchair came, and my seat was upgraded to 2A, business class, with a full bed. Wonderful. I was still feeling OK, but that may have been the painkillers and booze, but it all went downhill during the flight. I was hallucinating, full of fever and in some trouble.

As the plane landed, I was picked up by Rosie and taken directly to the Royal Berks hospital, where I spent the next three days quarantined, in and out of consciousness, with specialist doctors caring for me twenty-four hours a day.

I never did find out what spider bit me, but the little fucker did a good job.

Chapter 33

Who Wants a Napkin ?

I have another special memory from our Disney World adventure with Danni when she was just 9 years old. It was our final night in the enchanting world of Disney, and we were sitting in a lively restaurant, reliving the incredible time we'd had. The atmosphere was buzzing, and our food arrived just as our bellies started rumbling.

In all her excitement, Danni manages to spill something on herself. Being the dad I am, I decide to offer a little fatherly wisdom: "You see, that's why you should use a napkin. It's called a napkin for a reason." But Danni, with her quick wit and dry humour, fires back, "Oh really, is it because you put them on your nap?"

Disney World

Her snappy comeback caught me off guard, and I burst out laughing. The mouthful of beer I was enjoying at that moment had other plans. It gushed out at full speed, showering Danni's face, the table, and even the floor behind her. It was one of those instances where the unexpected and the hysterical collided, resulting in pure laughter and joy.

Disney World

For some inexplicable reason, this seemingly ordinary exchange became a treasured memory that we carry in our hearts. It's a story that never gets old, and we love to retell it, bursting into fits of laughter each time. While it may appear as a small incident, this memory will forever warm our hearts and bring smiles to our faces.

Chapter 34

My Premier League Debut

In 2006, Reading FC made their way into the Premier League, and boy, it was an exciting time! Ruth's school friend, Selby Armstrong, was offered the role of Kit Man for the club, and I received a phone call that changed my weekends forever. Selby asked if I'd like to take over his weekend gig as Kingsley Lion, the costumed mascot Lion of Reading FC. Of course, I couldn't say no – it was a fantastic opportunity, and I needed an assistant, so Garthy hopped on board almost as fast as I did, accepting the position. The gig paid £40 a game and as much Domino's pizza as we could stuff in our faces at halftime.

My role was to sign kids' shirts and entertain them before the match, during halftime, and after the game. I'd stroll around the pitch, mingle with the crowd, and have a laugh. But the absolute best part was getting to stand shoulder-to-shoulder with some of the biggest and best players in the world while in the tunnel and before the matches. They really are athletes and focused beyond the regular Sunday league I am used to. The tunnels are also exciting places to be, as I firmly believe that games can be won or lost even before a ball is kicked. Reading were new boys to the Premier League, so everything about the stadium, the fans and the boardroom atmosphere was electric. The players showcased their abilities for the first time on the big stage, shown worldwide. It was an amazing experience to be a part of, something I truly value as a life experience.

One time, during a match against Manchester United, I found myself in the tunnel with none other than Rooney – my all-time favourite player, a true Evertonian – and Ronaldo, who, in my opinion, is the best footballer to have ever graced the beautiful game. I couldn't help but notice how Ronaldo seemed to stand prouder and taller than any other player in the tunnel. His presence was just something else. He even went on to score two goals and secure the victory for United at 3-2. It was a sight to behold!

Another unforgettable moment was when Reading hosted Everton. Before the game, I stood in the tunnel wearing my full seven-foot-tall lion outfit in a Reading kit. I mustered the courage to approach David Moyes, Everton's longstanding manager, and pulled off an exaggerated "shhh" sign, bringing one finger from my paw to my lips. Then I unzipped my chest hair, revealing the Everton kit I was secretly wearing underneath. Moyes couldn't help but smirk. Goal achieved! I walked away with Leon Osman's shirt; it was a day to remember.

Life was full of incredible experiences, and I can't help but smile every time I look back on them.

Chapter 35

Park Villa for Life

Over the years, I have played for a few different clubs, each holding a special place for me. In every club, I made lifelong friends. It's a place where different backgrounds and ages all come together as teammates. Us against the world attitude... and if the team plays well, lads can be known for doing silly things!

Now, let me tell you about one of the tattoos that holds a special place in my heart – and it wasn't even on me. It was inked on our Park Villa football manager, Adam. You see, Adam was a true Park Villa devotee. It was a family affair, his dad's team, but they had experienced a heart-wrenching tragedy. A few years back, Adam's father had left the pitch in pain and was found lifeless in the changing room, having suffered a fatal heart attack. It was a devastating loss for the entire Park Villa community and many of his friends who played in the same team.

So, when the new season was about to kick off, Adam, Gregzy, and I, his two trusty centre-backs, were having a chat before a game. He came up with a challenge—a bet, really. He said, "Here's the deal, lads. If the two of you manage to score two goals each in any game this season, I'll get a tattoo of your choice."

Well, it didn't take long for this bet to be tested. Approximately 80 minutes into the first game of the season, with me standing over a free kick just outside the box, it looked like Adam was about to lose his bet. The final score? 4-0, with Gregzy putting away two goals and me bagging the other two. The game couldn't have ended any better for us.

A few months later, there we were, sitting next to Adam in a Benidorm tattoo parlour, with the entire team peering through the window to witness the spectacle. And what a legend Adam was! He went through with it and got "Acky" and "Gregzy" tattooed on him for life. It was a moment that cemented our bond, and it's a story we love to share and laugh about. A true testament to the camaraderie and good-natured banter that football can bring into your life.

Chapter 36

Boardroom to the Dojo

I've always been the kind of person people trust, and I tend to make friends quickly. Whether I'm walking into a pub and greeting everyone or strolling into trade shows and business meetings, folks just seem to want to spend time with me. I seem to have a natural knack for enjoying the world of business and the people in it. The hustle, the problem-solving, the relationships, the victories—it all gets my heart racing.

Over the years, I've dabbled in a few different businesses, and there have been no shortages of offers for business opportunities. People often want to invite me into their life stories, and I'm always open to a good adventure.

Take, for instance, Matt Fiddes from Matt Fiddes Martial Arts, a pretty interesting character. Back in the day when the King of Pop was in the UK, Matt was Michael Jackson's bodyguard. Matt and I chatted, and he took me aside to arrange a coffee meeting. He had this idea of me opening my very own martial arts schools and even taking the brand into the US. I dove right in with Gary, found US lawyers, and spent a good chunk of money on the legal paperwork.

The US has a crazy complex system with laws that vary by state. The due diligence and paperwork were enough to make your head spin. In the end, it didn't quite work out, but Matt was such a sport about it.

He added me to the master franchise communication group, kept me in the loop, and never asked me for a dime. He'd often call me to pick my brain or ask for advice. Danni and I even had the pleasure of meeting Matt and his wife, Monique, while we were on holiday once. This was Great for me, but amazing for Danni—meeting the big, big boss of her martial arts school, and him knowing her name and being so interested in her training and wellbeing.

Speaking of Danni, in her younger years, we wanted to get her into sports, activities, and groups, so she was put forward to try everything. Dancing, ballet, acting, gymnastics—all were OK, but nothing lit the spark until one day she fell into martial arts.

She excelled. She was a natural and continued to shine within the martial arts organisation. Winning National and International gold medals for a number of years. It was a mix of natural talent, grit, and determination that you can't ask from a girl aged between 7 and 17. All the instructors knew about her incredible skills, and we'd always joke that she had "won again." Along with her buddies Kayleigh, Tia, and Megan, the Reading girls practically cleaned up every trophy in sight for a few years.

The world of martial arts has been a fantastic part of our lives for over 10 years now and has also brought us even closer. It helped me teach a young Danni that commitment and hard work are necessary if you want to achieve special things in life, and with the right attitude and support, you can be the best in your chosen activity.

But here's a little something you might not expect: I managed to reach the pinnacle of earning a Black Belt in Taekwondo, too. Yep, you read that right. At around the age of 35, I started training alongside Danni and our friends. Danni, in her infinite wisdom, personally mentored me through each stage. She was my trainer at home, treating me like a 10 or 11-year-old. But by the time I hit 40, I proudly earned my Black Belt. It's one of my proudest achievements, and I wouldn't have done it without the support and guidance of my amazing little lady. The moment she awarded me with my Black belt can still bring me to emotional tears. It's such a proud moment in my life, not just because I achieved it but because we did it together. Dad and daughter were making another great team.

There are moments in life that still make me feel queasy to this day, like the time when Danni was just 10 years old. She was practising a very complex flying kick, and the adult instructor holding the pad didn't grip it firmly enough. Danni couldn't spring off it as intended, and instead, the youngster hit the floor face-first. Half of her brand-new front tooth went flying across the floor, and she let out a scream that still haunts me. Even thinking about it now gives me that sick feeling in the pit of my stomach. I've got a video of that moment, but I can't bring myself to watch it. We rushed to the dentist, and they fixed it a few weeks later. But not before she had to eat her Christmas dinner through a straw that year. Ugh.

But we were in it together, training martial arts side by side two to three nights every week. It meant the world to us, and it meant so much to Rosie and me that we both got two tattoos—one for each of her Black belts. We'd spend our weekends practising together, just like Everton, football, holidays, and everything else. It was our special bonding time, just me and my girl.

Now, Ruth didn't get too involved in the martial arts stuff. But she always made sure we were safe, together, having fun, and well-fed. She's the glue that holds us all together. On the other hand, I got to be the biggest child in the world and do my stuff. It's a cherished memory, and despite a few bumps and bruises along the way, it's a part of our journey that I wouldn't trade for anything.

Danni competing at the Great British Championships

Chapter 37

It's More Than a Game

Reflecting on the past, I can't help but think about how much football played a massive part in my life growing up and beyond. I'll admit I wasn't a football prodigy when I was younger. There were always better players on the field. I played for a pretty good team called Barton Rovers. We had some fantastic players like Neil Holloway, Andy Forbes, Gareth, and Alan. We were the first team under Neil's dad, Steve, and Mark Surtees as managers. We decided to change our kit to red and black stripes, and it was inspired by "Dennis the Menace," a comic we all loved as primary school kids.

Now, I may not have been one of the star players in the team until around the age of 13. But that's also when Garthy, Nelly, and the other better players left to play for Reading YTS. It didn't take long for me to step up my game. I can't tell you what changed, but I became the team captain by the time I was 15. I remained the captain of every football team I played for until I was 44, when I decided to hang up my boots.

Fox & Hounds FC

One significant moment in my football journey was when I started playing for Englefield at 14. I was small and young but was really good, with a great attitude. Something just clicked between the ages of 13 and 14, and it transformed my abilities on the field. Soon enough, I was skilled enough to get into an adult football team. Playing left-back, my brother Gary was right-back, and Mike held down the centre-back position. Everyone else was older, with Mike being the next youngest at 22 or 23.

I've always been a bit gobby on the football pitch, and that hasn't changed over the years. I knew my strengths—I was tenacious, consistent, and had decent skills for our level of play. I wasn't a world-class player, but I was good at my level. I never got benched from the age of 14 to 44, mainly because I played at the right level for my abilities.

One time during a game, I went up for a header, and this guy elbowed me square in the temple. It was a painful blow, but I managed to shake it off and get back on my feet. The guy who fouled me started berating me, saying, "What do you think you're doing at this level?" But I just laughed it off and shouted back.

Mid 20s football friends and my team

The next thing I knew, my brother Gary charged in and tackled the guy with force. After getting up, Gary proclaimed, "That's my brother. Leave him alone." But the guy wasn't finished yet. That's when Uncle Mike came charging in, and with his entire body, he smashed the guy to the ground. He sternly warned him, "He's my brother too. Touch him again, and I will kill you." The guy, quickly realising he was in over his head, huffed and puffed, asking if anyone else on the team was related to me. He failed to finish the half and went off the field, probably questioning his life choices. For us, football was more than just a game; it was a family affair. It brought us closer and taught us to look out for one another, on and off the field. And to this day, I can still hear Mike's voice echoing in my head, reminding me to be "good"—not just in football but in life.

Mikee was by far the best out of the three of us. He was a leader on and off the pitch and aggressive in the tackle. Nobody messed with Mikee on the pitch!

Chapter 38

In the Shadow of Genetics

I was in my early twenties when it came to our attention about something called Huntington's disease. It is a hereditary disease that is passed down from generation to generation. It's caused by a mutation in the HTT gene, which affects the brain's nerve cells over time. At first, it might seem like forgetfulness or mood swings, but as time goes on, it gets more serious. Problems with coordination, like stumbling or dropping things, and the final stages are the inability to walk or communicate. It basically shuts off communication between your brain and your body.

Either you have the gene, or you don't. If you have it, it's guaranteed that you will grow ill with Huntington's at some point in your life. If you don't, it is gone from your family line forever. Frightening, but it's as simple as that.

Dad chose to move to Spain when I was in my early twenties, I clearly remember him saying to me, "I've sold the house; you have three months to find somewhere to live".

Gary, Mike and I had recently found out that Dad also suffered from Huntington's, and he wanted to move to Spain to enjoy his retirement in the sun. he knew what happened to his Mum, so he wanted to live out his years with Ann somewhere beautiful.

Gary, Mike, and I discussed wanting to get tested ourselves, and since we all agreed and had our children, we went down the route. You must wait a minimum of 12 months after requesting a test with the hospital, and you must also go to a counsellor and speak with professionals.

The reason they gave was that it was incurable. Whether you receive a positive result or a negative one, it will certainly change your life forever. The odds are 50/50. Per child, no matter what... meaning Gary had a 50% chance, Mike had a 50% chance, and I had a 50% chance. We were told about negative guilt, where if you don't have it, you will feel guilty for any sibling who tested positive. It really was a big thing.

On March 12th 2014, almost a year after we inquired, Gary, Mike and I, together with our families, went in for the test, a bunch of physical and mental tests that the HD specialist at John Radcliffe Hospital understood. We were then called in one by one to talk to the specialist. We were all told we had 2 weeks to wait for the official blood test result. Although each of us was given a prognosis based on our physical tests, I was told they thought I would be positive (i.e. have it), Mike was told they thought he wouldn't, and Gary already thought he was showing signs.

The next two weeks were hard. It wasn't easy to concentrate on work at night; while lying in bed, my brain would focus on the possible impact on everyone. What would it mean to my family if I was positive? What would it mean to each of my brothers' families if they were positive? What if all three of us were? How will Pops be feeling, as he understands it's come from him? Would he feel guilt, even though It's out of his control? So many thoughts.

Two weeks later (April 1st – April Fool's Day, would you believe!), we were back in Oxford at the hospital. It was results day. We had all agreed that no matter what the results, we would stand by each other, help where needed, and most importantly, go for a beer together to talk about it immediately afterwards.

How naïve. It was far more emotionally involved than we all thought. It was life-changing. Gary went in first. He came out and said," Yeah, I have it. SHIT!" I think I went second, although it's a bit of a blur. I was told no, and Mike was also told no. We were both negative. Shock, guilt and confusion are all I can remember.

We drove to the pub for some lunch, as agreed. Although none of us wanted to be there, we all just experienced our own shock. During the drive, Ruth and I sat silently. We were clearly in shock, but I remember the song playing on the radio, Pharrell Williams, "Happy." I thought, fuck, I hope Gary isn't listening to this radio station!

Ruth and Sian wanted to probably celebrate for us, but they were also so sad for Gary and Delph. Unfortunately for Gary, the worry was just starting.

It's hard to explain how this felt, or what this means to a family, as most families hear bad news as it happens. For us, it was different; we heard that "in a few years", Gary would 100% come down with Huntington's and would most probably end up like our Nanna and how our Pops was going. Even writing this gets me so emotional. It's so sad.

Chapter 39

An Unseen Struggle

I n 2017, our family was hit by a thunderbolt from the clear blue sky. It was a year when the sun was shining, and the skies were as clear as our smiles. But beneath that cheerful facade, a tempest brewed, one that would shatter the tranquil surface of our lives.

We Ayckbourns had always been a tight-knit clan, weaving stories of joy, laughter, shared milestones, and unwavering support. Our lives were intricately woven together like a tapestry, and we cherished the togetherness. We had been through so much together, but none of us could have imagined the darkness behind the scenes.

Mike, my brother, had always been our rock, the one who held us together with his strength and a smile that could brighten even the gloomiest of days. But, behind that facade, he carried burdens none of us could fathom. Burdens that weighed him down and eroded his spirit in the shadows. Our family gatherings were still filled with laughter and celebrations, but there was a growing darkness concealed by our smiles. We were blind to the struggles Mike and his family were going through in secret. A tempest of pain and heartache they tried desperately to shield us from.

It was a peculiar paradox. We were a family built on openness and honesty, yet we were oblivious to the storm building within our own ranks. The layers of secrecy and the walls we'd built to protect each other were the very things that prevented us from seeing the truth.

In 2017, the truth came crashing down upon us, shattering the illusion of invincibility that had surrounded our family for so long. Mike was gone, and with his departure, the walls crumbled, revealing the painful realities he had kept hidden.

This is the story of that fateful year when grief entered our lives like an unwelcome guest, and we were forced to confront not only the loss of a beloved brother but also the profound secrets that had silently shaped our family's journey. It's a story of love, resilience, and the enduring strength of family bonds, even in the darkest shadows.

Chapter 40

A Farewell in Amsterdam

S unday, August 6th, 2017, a date forever etched in my memory, a day that would unknowingly become a pivotal chapter in my life. I was in Amsterdam for work and thought, "What a great excuse to catch up with Mike".

Little did I know that this would be our final encounter.

I remember knocking on his door that warm summer evening, looking forward to a cold beer or two and a good catch up. The thought of seeing Mike, my brother and confidant, always brought a sense of comfort, especially since he moved away. We shared a bond like few others, forged through the issues of our youth and time spent together while Pops was in his caravan.

Mike greeted me with his classic grin. We embraced, exchanged pleasantries, and laughed as if no time had passed since our last meeting. Little did I know this was the last "hello" we would ever say to each other.

We went straight out for a Chinese with his wife, Sian. Jack (their son) didn't come, and Mike made an excuse for him. A little strange, but nothing to think about. Throughout the dinner, Mike's curiosity began to surface through a few heartfelt questions. He asked about my well-being, my financial security, and, most importantly, whether I was genuinely happy with my path in life. At the time, I thought he was just being nosey and looking out for me, but in hindsight, he says something different.

Although subtle, Mike's inquisitions were a little deeper than normal. Inquiring about Ruth and Danni, he spoke with pride as he spoke of Danni's accomplishments in martial arts and told me to ensure she kept them up. He had an immense love for her, the kind only a father could muster. I remember feeling grateful and happy for his sincere interest in my life and the lives of those I held dear.

Mike was happy, fun and relaxed. At that moment, I didn't realise the depth of our conversation. We were simply catching up, enjoying each other's company over Chinese food and beers. It was a night filled with laughter and nostalgia. A night that, in hindsight, I'd come to cherish even more.

In retrospect, about six to nine months later, when the weight of Mike's absence had settled on my heart, I grasped the significance of that evening. He had been more than just an older brother; he had been a guardian, a protector, and an unyielding source of support. Mike had been looking out for me, ensuring I would be OK in the future.

As I revisited that heartfelt dinner and our deep conversations, it became clear that Mike's love went beyond mere words. It was in the concerned glances, the probing questions, and the genuine interest he showed. He had been saying his goodbyes in his own way, leaving me with memories of a bittersweet evening—a night that, now, I realise was the last time I would ever see my big brother.

Chapter 41

Where are You, Mikee?

Three days after our last encounter with Mike, we found ourselves in a state of anxiety that can only be described as palpable. Sian's frantic call to Gary sent shockwaves through our family. She was distraught because Mike had left abruptly, and the situation's urgency left us with no option but to dash to Amsterdam.

We were hurtling toward the unknown, but never in a million years did I think I was about to walk into what we did. Gary and I were the same on the flight over—very worried but more confused! What the hell could have happened!?

We landed in Amsterdam an hour later and drove straight to their house. Sian greeted us. She was broken and a complete wreak, resulting from a monumental argument between her and Mike. He left her with haunting words, promising that she would never see him again and that he would take his own life. "What... What are you saying? What happened, how" There were absolutely no clues as to what was unfolding in front of us.

Sian took his words seriously; in that moment, Gary and I were compelled to treat them with the utmost gravity. Shaking, we took action, launching a frantic search operation. It had been 24 hours since Mike's abrupt departure on that fateful Tuesday night, and there was no sign of him.

Throughout those harrowing 36 hours, we scoured the city twice. We visited every hospital and hotel and dashed from place to place in a state of frantic panic. We showed his photo to anyone who would listen, hunted for his car, and implored them to search their records for his name. Yet, our efforts seemed to lead nowhere.

It wasn't until Friday morning that a hotel contacted us with a crucial lead. The manager guided us to a room where Mike's clothes were neatly folded, his bag and laptop placed on top and an unsettling scene on the bed. At first, what appeared to be blood turned out to be red wine, a stark reminder of the distressing events unfolding. Packets of empty pill boxes were scattered about, bearing witness to Mike's anguish.

It was clear that Mike had made a desperate attempt to end his life but had somehow managed to awaken the following morning. The hotel staff showed us CCTV footage of him walking to his car early that morning. Gary and I instantly recognised him—our brother, consumed by sadness and in dire need of our support. It was a heart-wrenching moment, one that would forever change the course of our lives as we grappled with the profound pain that had enveloped him.

The hotel room, with its scattered clothes and empty pill boxes, told a tale of pain and despair. Mike had teetered on the edge, desperately attempting to escape the darkness that had engulfed him. But the universe, it seemed, said no.

As we watched the CCTV footage of his solitary walk to the car, a wave of emotions washed over us. Our brother, who had always been a pillar of strength, now stood before us as a man tormented by his demons. He was a person in need of help, but he had concealed his struggles so well that even his own brothers had been oblivious to the torment he had been experiencing.

We could only imagine the turmoil that must have plagued his mind as he wrestled with his pain. It was a cruel reminder that even those closest to us can suffer in silence, their anguish hidden behind smiles and laughter. Mike's cry for help had been a whisper in the wind, and we were determined to ensure it would not go unanswered.

We were resolute in our determination to bring him back from his despair. We just needed to find him.

Chapter 42

Behind Closed Doors

Returning to Mike's home after the startling discovery of his battle with despair, we sat down with Sian (Mike's wife). The pieces of a heart-breaking puzzle were falling into place, and it was a truth we had been utterly unaware of—a harsh reality concealed from us until now.

As we spoke with Sian, we learned of Jack's (their 14-year-old son) dark descent into the clutches of addiction. It was a road of self-destruction that left no drug untouched. The evidence lay before us, notebooks filled with cryptic lists and information, a testament to his involvement in drugs.

But the story ran deeper. Jack's issues had led to multiple involuntary commitments, the result of his increasingly erratic behaviour. He had spiralled into a world of chaos where nobody could help him. For Mike, his father, this must have been a most painful revelation—his own son somehow started to see him as the enemy.

I always saw Jack and Mike, just like Danni & I. Jack was Mike's world, but his world turned against him and his efforts to gain control.

My Nephew, Conor, and Niece, Alex, shared stories of Jack's regular escapades. Every week, while Mike was away for work, Jack would disappear into the night, only to return in the morning, often in the custody of the police. Sian's hourly calls to Mike during these tumultuous days and nights meant he had to leave his job constantly, attempting to manage the spiralling problem from afar. As I say, Jack was more than just his son; he was Mike's world, his "little man." Yet, he had lost Jack to the relentless grip of addiction, a nightmare that seemed to have no end.

Jack's struggles were not limited to substance abuse, but they helped him descend, unleashing on those around him. Sending him away for periods of time had become the only way to protect everyone involved, mostly Jack. Mike, a loving father who had always wanted the best for his son, must have felt like he was failing him. The mounting pressure and despair, mixed with other pressures must have reached a breaking point.

A chilling revelation came to light just days before the tumultuous argument that led to Mike's disappearance. Jack had climbed onto the ledge outside his bedroom window. It took the intervention of two Fire Fighters to restrain him, even resorting to handcuffing him to the window frame to prevent a tragic fall.

All of this was news to us, a series of revelations that shattered the illusions we had held dear. Only a few days earlier, the family had appeared to be in the highest spirits, the picture of happiness. The stark contrast between those moments and the harrowing truth that now confronted us left me bewildered, asking myself, "What the fuck was going on in our family?"

The truth about other issues, pressures and Jack's struggles, had left us reeling. It was as if a veil had been lifted, revealing the painful reality beneath the surface. The family we had known was in crisis, struggling under pressure and the chaos it had brought into their lives.

Mike's love for his son was unwavering. The pressure for Mike was coming from everywhere and I can only believe that he thought there was no way back and that he had lost him and his family life forever, and it became all-consuming. But that may just be me.

Pressure is something that only the person under it can understand. I know from personal experiences that you can easily start believing that things won't improve and that you will live forever in a spiralling hole with no means of escape.

It must have been a nightmare. The family was constantly alert, never knowing what the next day would bring. The family appeared so happy on the surface, but the battles they fought behind closed doors were a stark contrast.

In the days that followed, we were determined to seek answers and find a way to support Jack on his journey to recovery. It was a difficult road ahead, but we were committed to doing whatever it took to help him find his way out of the darkness. Our family bonds would be tested, but we remained resolute in our determination to overcome the challenges that lay before us.

Interpol, the renowned International Crime and Police force had tracked Mike's elusive journey through the country. His trail was marked by credit card transactions and car number plate sightings. Each report of a sighting became a frantic lifeline, propelling us into action as we sped to the locations where he had last been seen. Our hearts were gripped by desperation, yet we felt a crushing sense of helplessness.

We learned that Mike had stopped at a large hardware store similar to B&Q and then visited a fuel station to fill up his car. But then he vanished again into the enigmatic haze of uncertainty.

Thursday and Friday blurred together in a nightmarish continuum. With each passing moment, the horror of the situation intensified. Our ears were inundated with tales of Jack's spiralling descent, painting a portrait of a family torn apart by strife and discord.

The most chilling words came from Alex, who voiced a terrifying sentiment, "I knew he would do this; it was just a matter of time. He kept telling us he would kill himself." The revelation shook me to my core. How and why did nobody tell us?

Our emotions, shared but unspoken between Gary and me, swirled with turmoil and anger. We grappled with the same heart-wrenching question: How could this happen? Mike's silent cries for help were evident, yet his pride kept him from reaching out to anyone. In a world where the pressure proved too much to bear, he, like so many others, had become another mid-40s man pushed to the brink.

As the days passed, the search for Mike continued, and we were locked in a relentless battle against time and despair. Every moment without news of his whereabouts was excruciating.

Ruth's support was a source of solace, although she was more confused than I was.

While we were grappling with the terrifying possibility of losing Mike, Jack's well-being also remained at the forefront of our concerns. It was a family crisis of staggering proportions, and we were navigating uncharted territory. Drink and drug addiction had cast a dark shadow over our lives, and we were determined to confront it head-on.

We knew we had to tell Mum and Dad. Making that call to Dad was gut-wrenching. His voice trembled with shock and pain; his words unable to mask the depth of his anguish. It was a phone call etched in my memory forever, a moment that left me numbed by the magnitude of what we were facing. Nobody should have to tell a parent that their child was in such pain, and after days, we couldn't see a good outcome.

I boarded a flight back to the UK to deliver the news to Mum in person.

I had to. As I sat her and Titch down on her sofa, with me perched on the arm, an eerie silence settled in the room. Mum sensed the gravity of the situation, but the words remained unspoken. The atmosphere in that room was suffocating, and I couldn't speak. I knew I would carry the weight of that moment with me for the rest of my life.

Sunday evening, August 13th, brought a discovery that would forever haunt our souls. In a quiet corner of Germany, nestled in a carpark adjacent to a vast field, a dog walker stumbled upon a scene that would etch itself into the annals of our family's history.

There, alone in his car, Mike was found. The makeshift device he had crafted to cut the top off a BBQ gas cylinder had filled the confined space with lethal fumes. It was a tragic end to his struggle, one that left us broken to our cores. The emptiness that permeated the air was palpable, and our hearts ached with the weight of this unimaginable tragedy. No words will ever describe the feeling. You either know... or you're lucky.

A few weeks after that fateful August morning, the Dutch police delivered a haunting package to Gary and me at our office. It contained a chilling inventory of the belongings Mike had carried with him on his final journey—a package that held grim insights into his state of mind. Among the contents was a sizable knife. Really??

But the most haunting item was a list scrawled on the cardboard base of a gas canister cylinder. It was a chilling inventory of the numerous ways he had attempted to end his own life in the days leading up to that tragic day, along with heartfelt notes addressed to his family. In his words, he conveyed the depths of his despair and the anguish that had consumed him. If his chosen method had not succeeded, he revealed his intent to end his life through a different means... a knife that was destined to be sent to me.

The following months became a complete blur. Details of what transpired in Amsterdam, a city now forever intertwined with this tragedy, faded into a haze. I operated on autopilot as if my mind was shielding me from the depths of the pain. The passing of the next six to nine months felt like a distant memory, marked by an overwhelming melancholy and confusion.

I couldn't comprehend what had happened, and the weight of it all pressed down upon me, casting a shadow over my existence. Even six years later, the knowledge that Danni would never grow up knowing her uncle, the permanent void left by his absence, and the loss of his voice still felt surreal.

Chapter 43

In Memory of Mikee

On the Sunday night Mike passed away, I reached out to my closest friends—Garthy, Meikle, Bones, Nelly, Matty, all of whom are life-long friends mentioned in this book; and Gregzy, whom I got to know at 6th form. We soon became close, and he became part of the main group from then until this day.

They were all good friends of Mike, too; they grew up with him, played football with him, looked up to him, and drank with him. Within 20 minutes, they were all at my house, as if drawn by an unspoken bond of friendship and the weight of our collective grief. Together, we sat in the dimly lit kitchen, surrounded by the stillness of the night, and talked, shocked and all full of emotion. As for them, the significance unfolded as I explained what had been going on over the last week.

As the hours ticked by and the clock hands crept toward four or six in the morning, we found solace in each other's presence. We clinked glasses and shared stories, immersing ourselves in the memories of our dear Mike. He had been an integral part of our lives for each of us—a friend, a confidant, a source of laughter, and a wellspring of shared experiences.

Mike's passing struck a chord with us all, reminding us of the fragility of life and the enduring impact of the people we hold dear. He was not just a friend; he was a character, a unique soul who had left an indelible mark on each of our hearts. His charisma and charm were legendary, and his tough exterior only added to his mystique.

In those quiet hours of the night, we laughed and cried, and the room was filled with the echoes of Mike's stories and his larger-than-life presence. His absence was felt profoundly, but in our shared memories, we found a way to celebrate his life and keep his spirit alive. Mike was the kind of person you could never forget, and even as we mourned, we couldn't help but smile at the thought of the incredible journey he had taken us on.

Brother Mikee's Bench at my local park where I walk Maggie everyday

The day of Mike's funeral dawned, casting a solemn time over our hearts and the world around us. It was a day we had all been dreading, yet it was a day we needed to face together as a family and a community of friends.

The venue, a picturesque church nestled in Banbury, where Mike and his family had lived for several years previously, felt like a fitting place to bid our final farewell to a man who had touched our lives so profoundly. As we approached, we were met with a sea of faces, friends, and loved ones who had come to pay their respects, their sombre expressions reflecting the shared sense of loss. Inside the church, the atmosphere was hushed, heavy with the weight of our grief. The air was filled with the delicate fragrance of flowers adorning the altar, their vibrant colours a stark contrast to the sombre mood of the day.

One clear memory for me was seeing "Michael Ayckbourn" written on the gold plaque of his coffin. Indeed, a moment that hurt hard. Something I never expected to see, a single moment that still haunts me to this day.

The eulogy, delivered by Gary painted a vivid picture of his life—a life filled with laughter, adventure, and love. Stories and anecdotes flowed, each one a cherished memory of a man who had lived life to the fullest. Gary did well, something I know I don't have in me to do.

Tears welled in our eyes as we listened, and our hearts ached with the profound sense of loss. The words spoken during the eulogy captured the essence of Mike—the magnetic charisma, the unwavering loyalty, and the deep love he had for his family and friends.

The procession to the cemetery was a silent one, the only sounds the soft sobbing of mourners and the gentle hum of the car engines. The reality of Mike's absence settled in our hearts.

At the crematorium, we gathered one last time. Each of us took a moment to say our private goodbyes, express our love, and share our final thoughts with Mike. I waited until everyone left. I don't know why, but it just happened: me and him alone in the church. "Bye, Big Brother. I love you."

Following the solemnity of the crematorium, we found solace and celebration at the wake. Gary and I had chosen a golf club as the venue to honour Mike's memory—a place teeming with life and echoes of our brother's spirit.

Friends from near and far converged, transported by a fleet of coaches, to join in a gathering that swelled to hundreds. Les, a dear friend of Mike's, set the tone with tunes dear to him, spinning a soundtrack of 90's R&B, swing, Motown, and Soul that filled every room corner. Songs like Rappers Delight, New Edition, Blackstreet and Joe (Don't Wanna be a Player No More – his wedding song first dance!!)

It was a night of poignant duality; glasses raised in cheer, stories weaving through the crowd, evoking both chuckles and sobs—a fitting tribute to a man who touched so many lives.

Mikee's friends and family got together for a charity game of football after he passed away. Old players from Englefield (our club for years together), and old friends

The bar, generously stocked by Gary and me, kept the drinks flowing, a gesture of hospitality Mike would have appreciated. It was a night that truly celebrated Mike's journey—a final send-off that matched the breadth of his influence and the depth of our love. Gary and I split the bar bill; after receiving 3 cases of wine for free and a whole keg of beer, it still cost us £7,500 on drinks alone. Nobody had to put their hands in their pockets. Mike would have been proud of us for that.

Chapter 44

Navigating Loss and Aphantasia

I want to talk a bit about my feelings regarding Mike and some of the things we've been through with Pops. As I write this, 2022 has been a challenging year, and putting my thoughts into words has not been easy. But I've always believed you can't change the past. You deal with whatever life throws at you. It's time to start addressing a few things, I guess.

Mike's passing was incredibly tough. That phone call in Amsterdam felt like an endless nightmare. Every part of it has been painful, and it still hurts deeply. I almost got a tattoo a few months later to express how I felt. I had a vivid image in my mind: a large, black heart with a big piece cut away from the top corner and the black from inside the heart pouring out of it. That's how I felt, and if I think about it too much, I still feel.

Losing him was like losing a piece of my heart. But what's more heart-breaking is that he won't be here to witness all the important milestones in my and Danni's lives. He'll miss out on getting to know the person she is growing up to be. It's hard for me to accept that he won't see how much she's matured as an amazing young woman. Mike was such a cool guy, and he absolutely adored his family. I hate the thought that he won't be here to watch us grow and become the people I know he'd want us to be.

Mike was quite the character. He had a nightclub in Newbury, and he had more rhythm than anyone I've ever met. Honestly, he should have been born with soulful R&B background music playing at all times around him. He had a way with the ladies, and it seemed like he had a different girl every night – not one! He taught me a lot about life as a teenager. One of his golden pieces of advice was, "Make sure you're good because if you're good, all her mates will want you too." (Probably not the best advice, but it worked for a while).

What has always bothered me is that I can't picture memories.

I remember fun and sorrow, but not vividly or easily. I thought everyone was like this until late 2022 when I watched a TikTok video about Aphantasia - A condition that causes a lack of visual memory. I watch another video, and another, each time taking tests for myself. I then became obsessed with visiting NHS and specialist websites and taking more tests. Fuck, I have Aphantasia. I literally see black when I close my eyes. If someone says to close their eyes and picture a red apple or a star, people can do so. I can't. I see black.

It broke me again. I honestly thought everyone saw like me, but no, when others think of past memories, they can vividly see them to some extent. Not me. I see nothing.

This is actually hard to take when you have lost someone so close. As the days and years go by, I hate myself for not being able to see us talking, playing together, and having a laugh. But it's impossible for me; I see nothing.

Chapter 45

Lockdown Diaries

Lockdown:- It's a word that sends shivers down most people's spines, it was a horrific time for many. But you know what? Personally, I loved every single second of it. The whole summer was scorching hot, beautiful weather, and I got to be at home while the business was humming along, growing faster than ever. Everyone was stuck at home; you won't believe how many more toys people ordered. It was like Christmas every day.

All I had to do was sit in the garden with Danni and Maggie (my four-legged best friend) and make silly dance videos on this new craze app called TikTok. It was the hottest thing on the internet, and we just jumped right in. Danni and I became TikTok sensations overnight. Our videos took off like a rocket, and we found our niche, with all the "mums"' loving us. Soon, the followers came pouring in, and before I knew it, our videos were reaching 2 million views, and we had over 50,000 followers. Personally, I think Maggie was the real star of our videos, but my silly, odd socks might have had something to do with it.

But lockdown wasn't just about dancing and having fun. I also managed to carve out some "me time." Tom at the Fox & Hounds, bless his heart, allowed me to sneak in twice a week for a pint. And Adam, the fitness fanatic, at Shredquarters gym, agreed to give me some 1-2-1 training. That guy is one of the most driven people I know, but he's got this laser focus on one thing at a time. So, he came to me seeking advice on growing his business, and he wanted to take the franchise route.

Now, gyms had it tough during the lockdown, and Adam needed a hand. He asked for 20 grand, and I'll admit I was pretty close to lending it to him. Almost. But in the end, we all made it through, and we made lockdown a time for growth, both personally and in our businesses. It was like one big holiday, and as I mentioned, I even squeezed in a couple of "work" trips to Antigua and Bermuda. It's funny how sometimes the worst situations can become opportunities for something wonderful.

On the flip side, when I think back on the negatives from the lockdown, it's frightening how the world went into complete panic mode, and understandably.

Nobody knew what COVID-19 was and how many millions it would kill. Although I had a great time at home, it was my last trip to China and most definitely my last trip to see Wendy, Simon, and the rest of my team at the factory in Zhuhai. Again, it was something that ended without warning.

Everyone was scared, we wouldn't open our doors, people became isolated, and the mental health impact on everyone was huge. I was old enough to understand what was important, but it was completely switched off for Danni and her friends – no more seeing each other, no face-to-face communication. It definitely put children of all ages back a couple of years compared to our days of growing up.

Chapter 46

Gym, Design Agency, What's Next?

L et me take you back to the moment when the idea of opening my very own Shredquarters Gym franchise was just a seed, a seed that would soon grow into something quite extraordinary. It all started one evening while I was at a gym class, doing my best to stay in shape. That's when Adam, the instructor, turned to me and popped the big question, "Hey, do you fancy buying into a franchise?" I was there with my good mate Clive (Craig still kicks himself for training that night). But there I was, presented with an opportunity. I was told that the Guildford location was all set to open, but there was a little hiccup - the manager had backed out. Now, you know me, always up for an adventure. I thought, "Alright, this sounds interesting, but I don't know the first thing about running a gym." So, I turned to Clive and asked, ""Fancy going 50/50 on this one?"

Why not" was his simple reply... I like that!

That night, I went home and remember standing in the shower, thinking about this whole thing. I mean, I know business, but I'm clueless about gyms. More importantly, I don't have the time to run one. I've got my other businesses to manage.

By now, I have Concept to Consumer, the design and creative agency I've been running for a few years. It's my baby. Knowing so little about the fitness world, I pondered how I could ever make a gym business work.

And as if by divine intervention, Adam had the same concerns. He wasn't sure we could juggle this new venture with our other commitments. But then, we both had this lightbulb moment—if Clive and I teamed up with one of the instructors, it would just work. (Kieran, a dedicated instructor at the gym, was willing to pitch in and believed in our vision.) And just like that, we opened our very own Shredquarters Gym franchise in Guildford three months later.

Things were going pretty well at first. It had the potential to be something amazing. But then, Kieran, he just wasn't the right fit. He didn't quite grasp the bigger picture and wasn't too keen on taking direction. I've always believed in putting in that extra effort and working harder than the rest, but Kieran had a different approach. So, while the gym did alright, it wasn't the resounding success it could have been. We set it up and launched our gym business in Guildford in early 2022. Sometimes, things don't work out as planned, but you live and learn. We still have it now, but it just ticks along.

Chapter 47

Resilience in Lockdown

The summer of 2020 arrived amidst the backdrop of a world grappling with the challenges posed by the COVID-19 pandemic. For many, it was a time marked by uncertainty and isolation, but within our family, it became a period of unexpected bonding and resilience.

Life as we knew it had come to a standstill with the lockdown in full swing. But instead of succumbing to the boredom and monotony that often accompanies such situations, we found a silver lining. My daughter Danni, then 13-14 years old, and I seized the opportunity to make the most of our time together. Every day became a holiday, a chance to create memories that would last a lifetime.

The laughter and creativity that flowed during those moments provided a much-needed escape from the grim realities of the outside world.

My partner, Ruth, worked tirelessly during this period. Her dedication to her role in the school extended beyond the call of duty. She was there every day, including weekends and holidays, providing essential support during a time when educational institutions were navigating uncharted waters.

Amidst the challenges of the pandemic, a glimmer of hope shone through in the form of our toy business. Against all odds, it turned out to be our best year to date, and we achieved the remarkable milestone of selling $20,000,000+ worth of products, including over 3,000,000 Durex bullets to over 27 countries. It was a testament to our team's resilience and the unwavering support of our customers during a time of upheaval.

However, the summer of 2020 held another significant milestone for us. As I mentioned, we launched Concept to Consumer Ltd, a design and branding agency. This venture allowed us to unleash our creative energies, giving birth to brands like AthPleasure and Airwaves. It was a new chapter in our journey, a testament to our adaptability and the spirit of innovation that had always driven us forward.

Chapter 48

Navigating the Storm

The year 2021 arrived with its own challenges, testing our resilience and adaptability as a family and business owners. Little did we know that the ensuing months would plunge us into a whirlwind of unprecedented events that would reshape the landscape of both our personal and professional lives.

I spent most of that year dealing with global component shortages. During COVID, the world started to shut down. Lockdowns, supply chain disruptions, and a general atmosphere of uncertainty permeated every facet of our business. It became daunting to keep our operations afloat amid the chaos, and each day seemed to bring a new set of obstacles to overcome.

The pandemic affected every business sector imaginable, causing a ripple effect that, in turn, caused prices to skyrocket across various industries. The world had changed dramatically, and we found ourselves navigating uncharted waters. What once felt like a steady ship now seemed like a fragile vessel tossed about in a storm of economic turbulence.

One of the most striking manifestations of this upheaval was the astonishing increase in container ship prices. What was once a routine cost of $6,000 had ballooned to an astronomical $30,000. This seismic shift rippled through our supply chain, threatening the very foundation of our business. The once reliable logistics and transportation systems now posed challenges we had never anticipated. Containers were being left portside for months without being collected. The world was starting to see what happens when people can't do their jobs.

As we grappled with the soaring costs and logistical nightmares, it became evident that adaptability was a desirable trait and a survival imperative. The strategies that had served us well in the past were rendered obsolete, and we had to quickly evolve to meet the demands of this new and unpredictable business landscape.

To make matters worse, the already strained shipping industry struggled with a shortage of staff to unload these precious cargo vessels. The ripple effect continued, creating a domino reaction of delays and disruptions that impacted businesses worldwide. Customers eagerly awaited our products, which languished in shipping containers stranded at sea or piled up at congested ports. The logistical nightmare seemed insurmountable, and we found ourselves grappling not only with the financial implications but also with the growing frustration of our loyal customers.

Chapter 49

The Face of Adversity

During that time, our family faced a personal crisis. In the summer of 2021, Ruth received an abnormal smear test result, a major concern. The subsequent diagnosis was swift and heart-wrenching—cervical cancer. The news sent shockwaves through our lives, and the weight of business challenges suddenly paled in comparison to the battle that lay ahead for Ruth.

Ruth faced the battle of her life with the same fighting spirit she had always had. Two surgeries followed, each a testament to her strength inside and out. As Ruth navigated the uncertain waters of cancer treatment, we decided not to let others know. Let's see what the outcome is first, she kept telling me.

By November 2021, she had received the welcome news of clearance, marking a victory against a formidable adversary. The battles, both in the business arena and personal front, had left indelible marks on our family.

The emotional and psychological impact was deep and hit amazingly hard. It shocked me to think that there was a chance that we wouldn't grow old together. Or that Rosie may pass away before me... both thoughts kept me awake at night.

Maybe because I had been too "busy" for the last 18 years to think about our health, and after my Huntington's clearance, as far as I was concerned, we would grow old. Again, how naive...

I wish this was the only cancer story during this time in our lives, but I'm sorry to say that less than a month later, we had another casualty.

Chapter 50

Navigating Business Shifts and Personal Trials

A s the summer of 2021 unfolded, it also marked the beginning of the end of an era that has filled my life for 20 years.

Lee, our trusted business partner, expressed his desire to retire. This was a transition that would bring both challenges and opportunities. The dynamics of our business partnership, which had been integral to our journey, were evolving, and we faced a future that held both uncertainty and the promise of new beginnings with the chains released. Lee was excellent in the first few years, but he became impossible. Rude, lying, and manipulative. Nobody in the team in China liked him, but he was their boss, and he made sure they knew it with an iron fist and zero respect. He held us back over the last six to seven years, but we grew year on year in sales and profits despite him.

From October 2021 to March 2022, a significant chapter unfolded in our business journey—a chapter marked by ambition, opportunity, and, ultimately, a bitter disappointment.

During this time frame, we had a promising prospect on the horizon. We had identified investors who saw the true value of our business, assessing it at a substantial $20,000,000 -$25,000,000.

It was a momentous opportunity that held the potential to reshape our company's and personal futures. The plan was ambitious yet promising—we aimed to buy out our long-time partner, Lee, and take full control of the entire design and manufacturing business, including all the China staff. And Lee got to retire, happily.

This transition wasn't just about numbers and financial transactions; it was about the prospect of taking the reins and steering our business into a new era. There were also about 350 dedicated staff members in China, individuals whose livelihoods were tied to the success of our enterprise. We were determined to make this venture a resounding success, not only for ourselves but for every member of our extended family who relied on us.

However, as the deal progressed, we encountered unforeseen challenges. Lee's actions and decisions during this crucial period cast a shadow of doubt over the entire endeavour. He provided us with false figures and frustratingly refused to disclose the financial information that would enable the investors to commit to the deal. Our best-laid plans began to unravel.

The disappointment was palpable, a bitter taste of unfulfilled potential and dashed dreams. We had seen a path forward that would have undoubtedly led to new heights for our business and team. Yet, despite our best efforts and unwavering commitment, the deal ultimately broke down because of one man's greed.

This chapter reminds us that opportunities can be fleeting in the world of business, and challenges can arise from unexpected corners. It was a period of profound learning and adjustment, the intricate and unpredictable terrain of entrepreneurship.

Chapter 51

Strength in Unity

December 2021 brought with it another heart-wrenching revelation—a diagnosis that would change the course of our lives once again. Roger, Ruth's dad, received the devastating news that he had Oesophagus cancer.

The journey that lay ahead was arduous and fraught with uncertainty. With the diagnosis, a battle began, one that would test Roger's strength and resilience, as well as the unwavering support of our family.

In early 2022, Roger embarked on a challenging path of chemotherapy. It was a gruelling regimen, marked by its physical and emotional pains. Yet, with each session, he demonstrated a remarkable determination to confront it head-on.

As the seasons turned, the summer of 2022 brought a pivotal moment in Roger's battle against cancer—the operation. It was a significant milestone, a testament to his courage and the dedication of the medical professionals who stood by him. The procedure marked a critical moment in his journey toward recovery.

The summer of 2022 also saw the resumption of chemotherapy, which continued through the late summer and into the fall. Once again, Roger faced the daunting challenge of enduring the treatment's side effects while clinging to the hope of a brighter tomorrow.

Our family rallied around Roger throughout this period, offering support and love. It was a time of shared strength and unity, a testament to the bonds that held us together in the face of adversity.

A few months after Roger's successful operation, he wanted to start getting fit for golf again.

What a hero. So, he joined the same gym as Danni, and they both visited together, with her showing him what exercises to do. They were probably the youngest and definitely the oldest members during each gym visit. How amazing that a 16-year-old would take her Grandad (her DurDur,) to the gym. They both made me proud, and Roger worked so hard to get fit that he managed the Egypt golf holiday with his mates in 2023.

Chapter 52

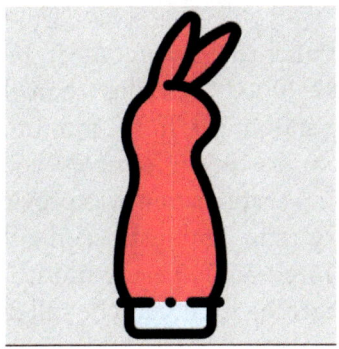

The Fight for our Business Legacy

April 2022 marked the beginning of nearly two years that would forever alter the course of our lives. This time was marred by betrayal, deceit, and an unrelenting legal battle that cost us every penny and over $2,000,000 in legal fees.

On April 5th, a day that will be etched into my memory with bitterness, Lee committed an act of treachery that defied comprehension. In a stunning turn of events, he seized control of our beloved business, which we had nurtured and grown over two decades. It was a theft of not just property and assets but also trust and the reputation we had painstakingly built in our industry.

Lies, ego, and greed served as the driving forces behind this shocking betrayal. In the blink of an eye, our entire successful business had been snatched away, leaving us in disbelief and despair. The industry in which I had invested 20 years of my life now bore the stains of baseless accusations and insinuations. The saying, "There is no smoke without fire,"" haunted us as people questioned our integrity, unaware of the truth hidden beneath the surface.

In his pursuit of personal gain, Lee initiated a lawsuit against Gary and me, targeting us personally. It was a ruthless tactic, an attempt to bully us into submission and strip us of everything we had worked tirelessly to achieve over two decades. His actions were nothing short of an assault on our livelihoods, dreams, and identities as entrepreneurs. If we did nothing, Lee would have also taken our houses and any savings we had. He was trying to ruin our families as well as us.

Lee saw the investment offer to Gary and me to buy him out and wanted the whole thing. All $25,000,000, rather than the $4,000,000 we had together calculated that should get. In the months before April, his greed went from $4,000,000 to "I won't agree unless you give me an additional $2,000,000." No reason or explanation was provided. In the end, we offered him $7,500,000 to retire and just become the landlord; we would then continue to pay him $80,000 every month in rent. He would be raking it in and doing nothing for it. And he still owned the land.

We, however, would pocket a couple of million and use the rest as an investment into future growth. But Lee's ego wouldn't allow it. He would rather ruin it for everyone if he wasn't winning far more than everyone else.

In response, we chose not to cower in the face of adversity. Instead, we counter-sued with a claim of $25,000,000, a resolute stance that we would fight to protect what was rightfully ours. The battle lines were drawn, and we were prepared to give everything we had to seek justice and reclaim our stolen legacy.

Little did we know that this would mark the start of the darkest and most challenging two years of my life, a year in which the very foundations of trust and honour were shaken to their core.

Chapter 53

Auntie Joan

I n 2022, our family got some more tough news—Ruth's Auntie Joan was diagnosed with womb cancer. This worried everyone in our close family, and we knew we needed to stick together to help her through it.

Auntie Joan, a really strong lady, faced her sickness with a tough attitude. Even when she had pain and bleeding, she didn't talk much about it. Joan thought her tough times were just because she grew up in a time when life was even harder. Auntie showed she was strong like the people from her generation, used to dealing with tough stuff without needing sympathy.

Even though Auntie Joan kept a lot of her struggles private, she went through a brave journey of treatments for almost a year. Unfortunately, she lost her battle in October 2023. So sad for her closest family and everyone involved.

Chapter 54

Farewell Pops

During what had been the hardest and most challenging year possible for our household, in August 2022, our attention shifted to another deeply personal and heart-wrenching decision. Dad, my Pops, our patriarch, found himself in the final stages of Huntington's Disease. A rapid and irreversible decline in his health over the past year meant that he was barely able to communicate and unable to feed himself or sit up by himself any longer. Faced with the stark reality of his condition, he made a courageous choice—to embrace euthanasia to end his suffering.

This choice was only made available to him six months earlier when the Spanish government legalised euthanasia. It was a long, tedious, and frustrating journey, as it was so new, but one worth taking.

The Spanish medical system was labyrinthine, fraught with complexity and lacking emotional construct. Our personal path demanded a harrowing task, where I had to record a video of Dad asking him the agonising questions that would determine his final wish. His bravery shone through as he faced these difficult conversations.

I loved Dad for his tough decisions, but I loved and respected him just as much for his positive attitude. When I flew to Spain to make the video for the doctors, I walked into his house with a quick kiss and a cuddle and told him I wanted to complete the video as efficiently and thoughtfully as possible. "It must be serious, Dad, as it's going to the doctor to decide if they will allow you to make this decision yourself" I then explained to him and Ann that I had researched and googled euthanasia a great deal in the UK and had prepared a list of specific questions that were asked during every procedure in the UK.

"OK, are you ready to start?" I said.

"First question I've been told to ask... Has your Dog been neutered?"

He looked at me, and a huge smile came over his face; he burst out laughing, which made us all laugh so much we were crying. Unfortunately, Dad was probably too ill to laugh so much that he started choking badly. "You can't die yet, Dad, I haven't finished the questions.". A few minutes later, we all composed ourselves again. I love that we had that silly moment. It reminds me of an old saying I love: *Just because I make light of a situation doesn't mean I take it lightly.*

Week after week, we waited for the authorisation to allow us to travel to Spain for the procedure. The legality of euthanasia in Spain was still in its infancy, making this process all the more challenging and unfamiliar for everyone involved.

As the sands of time trickled by, the weight of these situations bore down upon our family. One was a testament to strength and the enduring spirit of life, while the other was a heart-rending farewell to a loved one. It was a poignant reminder that life, with all its beauty and pain, continues to unfold, pushing us to confront the depths of our emotions and the complexity of our choices.

For nearly two years, a disquieting silence hung heavy between Dad and Gary, two pillars of our family. Their estrangement was marked by an absence of phone calls or contact, a void that seemed insurmountable. In the middle of this painful chasm, I found myself torn between the two men I loved dearly.

Dad had made a decision, a heart-wrenching one at that—he had chosen to turn away from Gary and wanted nothing to do with him in his final days. The reasons behind this decision were complex and weighed heavily on all of us. Dad thought Gary never called or communicated, which was true. To Gary, Dad was not the source of the estrangement; instead, he blamed Ann, our Step-mum. It was a tangled web of emotions, accusations, and resentment that threatened to engulf our family. It had gone too far for either of them to call the other, so they only had my updates.

Chapter 55

Bridging the Divide

C aught in the middle of this horrible situation, I found myself in the unenviable position of being the intermediary. I cajoled Gary to reach out to Dad to mend the fractures that had torn them apart. Simultaneously, I implored Dad to reconsider, open his heart, and forgive, even for a fleeting moment.

I understood the gravity of Dad's sentiments, the pain and frustration that had festered over the years. His resolve to distance himself from Gary stemmed from a place of self-preservation. Huntington's disease, a cruel spectre that loomed over Gary's future, made it agonisingly difficult for him to witness Dad's deteriorating health. It was as if he were staring into the abyss of his own destiny, and it terrified him.

In my efforts to bridge the divide, I flew over to see Dad on several occasions. One such visit brought Gary along, but his presence was short-lived. He refused to stay at Dad's home, limiting his interaction to just a few hours. We landed, I hurried to Dad's house while Gary checked into a hotel in town. We spun a tale about planning to fly in the following morning, but fate had other plans. At 5 a.m., he tested positive for COVID-19, shattering the illusion of the potential reunion I was looking forward to so much. If I'm being honest, he seemed secretly relieved, as it gave him a reason to evade the visit. Clearly, he was yearning for a night out, a break from the emotional turmoil.

I empathised with Gary's fears and anxieties, aware of the torment that lurked beneath the surface. I was on my own emotional journey, plus grappling with the weight of my father's anger and disappointment in Gary's prolonged absence. The burden of bearing witness to this fractured family dynamic and needing to conceal the truth from everyone involved weighed heavily on me. Especially as I knew Dad wasn't long for this earth. We only had to see, speak, and hug him a few more times. He had already lost one son, please, not another.

In these moments of turmoil, family bonds were stretched to their limits. The chasm between my brother and dad seemed insurmountable, and I stood helplessly in the middle, yearning for reconciliation from either side. Once broken, bridges can be challenging to rebuild. People can be stubborn – as they say, you can take a horse to water, but you can't make it drink!

Chapter 56

Final Goodbyes

November 2022 marked a pivotal moment in our family that would forever etch itself into our memory.

Danni, my compassionate daughter, came to me with a solemn request—she wanted to visit her Pops, her beloved grandfather, for what she knew would be their last meeting. Her words hung heavy in the air, and I knew this was a moment of profound significance.

I relayed Danni's wish to Dad and Gary separately, extending an invitation to both of them to join us together. The prospect of saying their final farewells loomed, and I hoped the shared experience would bridge the gap forever.

However, it took Gary two agonising weeks to confirm his desire to come along, and even then, it was only when I took the initiative to book our tickets for a few days that he followed suit.

We travelled over, and Danni and I stayed at their home, while Gary, Bethyn, and Ciara stayed in a hotel in town.

I can only speak personally, but I felt so much pride for Danni; she acted maturely well beyond her years as we sat through the night talking and laughing at Pops. I watched closely over her and saw that she was looking at him, remembering, taking it in. Gary and the girls came for an hour to say their goodbyes, but for us, it was different. We understood the seriousness of what we were there for. For Pop's grandchildren to say goodbye to him forever.

Pops could see, too. They knew Danni was seconds away from tears at every moment, but as we all joked and laughed into the night, we knew it was a special moment.

It was Titch, my Stepdad, who seemed to understand the importance of the position I was being put in more than anyone else. He was clearly upset and wanted to offer help, but he knew he had to stay out of it.

In this poignant moment, he expressed genuine emotion and acknowledged the gravity of what we all endured. Titch spoke of his profound respect for Dad's courageous decision, which few could comprehend without first-hand experience. He recognised the bravery it took to make such a choice and spoke openly about how he had thought for many hours about the horrible situation.

At this juncture, we were acutely aware that Dad's time with us was measured in days, weeks, or at most a few months away. Titch's unexpected display of empathy and compassion supported me, Ruth, and Danni, by extending a hand of understanding and care when we needed it most. It was a poignant reminder that beneath the surface of our family's struggles and conflicts existed the potential for moments of unexpected connection and thoughtful understanding.

Chapter 57

In the Shadow of Legal Storms

The relentless legal battle with Lee cast a long and ominous shadow. Our once-thriving business, culminating in two decades of hard work and dedication, lay dormant and shuttered. The fallout was immediate and profound, leaving us grappling with the abrupt halt of a life we had known for so long.

The ceaseless legal proceedings were all-encompassing, consuming our waking moment. Our ability to communicate with the outside world was stifled, and the vibrant business we had built from the ground up was brought to a standstill.

Yet, the hardships did not end there. The financial burden of the legal battle bore down upon us with unrelenting force. Our monthly expenses soared to a staggering $120,000, an unyielding drain on the savings we had carefully amassed over the years. What was once a nest egg of over $1,500,000 slowly dwindled under the relentless pressure.

By February 2023, we had already exhausted $1,500,000 of our own funds, and the business, once flush with resources, teetered on the precipice of financial ruin. This financial strain took an immeasurable toll on our family as we grappled not only with the emotional weight of our circumstances but also with the daunting reality of mounting debts and dwindling resources.

During this tumultuous period, we were forced to confront the harsh reality that our very livelihoods, built painstakingly over the course of two decades, hung precariously in the balance. The road ahead remained uncertain, and the financial and emotional toll of our legal battles weighed heavily upon us all.

This was a hugely lonely time for me. I couldn't let everyone know how I was feeling, as I had to continue to be the "'father'", the "man of the house" who brings home security to his family. I couldn't speak to Gary about what I was going through as he had personal issues. So, every morning, every night, the pressure weighed me down.

Outwardly, I kept a positive face and attitude, but inside I knew that everything I had worked so hard to achieve was being stolen away, and I could do nothing about it. Had I failed as a partner? Had I failed as a father? Thoughts that had never come to mind before were hitting me far too frequently. But I knew my attitude would never die... I knew I just had to keep moving forward daily, and I would get outside the troubles and back onto solid ground.

Amid the chaos of legal battles and financial strain, a glimmer of hope emerged on the horizon. Individuals expressed a keen interest in investing in our design agency business, Concept to Consumer Ltd. The prospect of infusing new capital and potential growth into our venture promised a brighter future.

However, the cruel twist of fate that had befallen us was again at play. Like a relentless storm, the legal case that had brought our lives to a screeching halt continued to dictate the terms of our existence. We were informed that we had to defer these investment opportunities until our legal battle was resolved.

Once more, dreams and aspirations were put on hold. The prospect of expansion and growth for our business, a beacon of hope during trying times, remained tantalisingly out of reach. The rollercoaster of uncertainty persisted as we navigated the turbulent waters of the legal arena, watching as potential opportunities slipped through our fingers.

Chapter 58

Celebration Amidst Adversity

I t was November 2022, a month that bore witness to an exciting milestone for The Shredquarters, a testament to a great launch, and Adam's fantastic attitude. The news had arrived that we had been shortlisted for the prestigious title of 'Gym of the Year.' This accolade, an emblem of excellence within the fitness industry, held the promise of further validation for all the hard work and commitment that had gone into shaping The Shredquarters into the exceptional facility it had become.

Eager to embrace this momentous occasion, we wasted no time in booking a table at the grand Gym Awards ceremony set to take place in Leicester. The timing of the event was fortuitous, as it coincided with my return from our poignant trip to Spain to visit Dad with Danni. It was an exhilarating journey, transitioning from one deeply emotional experience to a night of celebration and recognition.

The evening unfolded in a whirlwind of excitement and anticipation. Surrounded by fellow fitness enthusiasts and industry professionals, the atmosphere was charged with the collective energy of those who shared a passion for health and wellness. Though the ultimate prize eluded us, as we did not secure the title of "Gym of the Year," the sheer fact that we had been selected as finalists was a victory in itself—an achievement that filled us with pride and gratitude.

Amid life's challenges, we found joy in this moment of recognition. It reminded us that there were still moments of celebration and affirmation within the trials and tribulations.

As we reflected on the night, we were reminded that success is not always measured by the awards on the shelf but by the journey, the impact on the community, and the passion that fuels every endeavour. The Shredquarters, though not crowned "Gym of the Year," had triumphed in its own right—a source of inspiration for all who walked through its doors and a place to forget all your troubles for an hour.

Chapter 59

Titch Sudden Goodbye

December 2022, Titch, my stepdad, had fallen. He was in a bad way, and an ambulance was en route to their house. As I arrived at their home, the gravity of the situation became painfully evident. There he lay, weak and vulnerable, in the hallway of his own home. It was a sight that filled me with dread, and I knew that as such a big man, this was not going to be good. He looked in a bad way too, barely awake, with Mum with a look of panic and worry in her eyes.

Hours ticked away, fraught with tension. Two ambulances and four crew members later, we finally managed to get Titch admitted to the hospital.

It had taken most of the day, as the machines on both ambulances weren't working. The source of his ailment was a seemingly innocuous ulcer on his ankle, but it had become a breeding ground for infection. Sepsis had taken hold, causing his organs to shut down.

That evening brought the grim prognosis that no family ever wishes to hear: Titch wouldn't make it through the morning. The gravity of the situation was crushing, and the weight of despair was clear to Mum, by now a broken shell, consumed with dread. How could this happen so quickly? Covid had its toll on Titch, as he needed to keep active, but the lockdown only ensured that he was stuck in his chair 99% of the time. I always remember Titch joking about how he had kept the same £10 note in his pocket for over 2 years during lockdown – that made him proud! Haha.

Mum was in total shock, and we both knew I had to call Kathryn and Gareth, my stepbrother and sister, and alert them to the urgency of the situation. Time was of the essence, and I knew they needed to be by Titch's side. Although they live on the southwest coast of Wales, it's a 3–4 hour drive.

I had already called them earlier that day, and they were planning on coming up in the morning, but this was urgent.

What followed was a week of indescribable hardship. We attempted to sleep in the uncomfortable chairs of the hospital waiting room, hearing the nonstop sounds of a hospital ward. Our lives were temporarily put on hold as we took turns staying with Titch. The emotional toll was immeasurable as we grappled with the uncertainty of whether he would pull through.

Despite the profound sorrow and anxiety that enveloped us, an unexpected blessing emerged from the darkness. We drew closer as a family than ever before, and the shared experience of confronting this brought us together in ways we couldn't have anticipated.

On December 21st, we received the news that Titch was moved to the Sue Ryder Hospice at Prospect Park. We knew what this meant, and it was still so unbelievable. There was no way I was about to lose both my dads in a matter of weeks. Titch has been my second dad since I was five.

Sue Ryder is a special place where angels work, but unfortunately, we all knew his time was quickly coming to an end. Titch passed away at lunchtime on December 22nd 2022, with Mum and Kathryn by his side.

Who would have thought that only a week before, I was talking to Titch about my dad passing away soon. With him being so comforting and emotional to me, explaining how sad the whole situation was, only a few days later, he himself would be the one to pass away. The two fathers in my life were gone, when selfishly, I probably needed them most.

In the wake of Titch's passing, the days became months that stretched like an unending labyrinth of grief. The toll on Mum was unmistakable;

her once vibrant spirit had been eclipsed by a profound sense of loss. She moved through life with an air of desolation, her demeanour reflecting the depths of her sadness. It was a painful and heart-wrenching transformation to witness.

As I found myself in a unique position, not occupied by the demands of work, I dedicated myself to providing Mum with unwavering support. The responsibilities of managing finances, handling the practicalities of life, and simply being there to keep her company became my daily focus. It was a daunting and exhausting process for us both, but it was a path we needed to walk together.

Time, as it often does, played a pivotal role in our journey of healing. With each passing month, Mum's grief began to shift and evolve. The acute pain began to soften, replaced by a sense of melancholy that was more manageable. While the loss of Titch remained a constant ache in our hearts, time offered us a glimmer of solace.

Yet, amid this gradual process of healing, there was a looming shadow of uncertainty. Titch's decision not to take the 25% tax-free option from his pensions had left Mum in a state of financial apprehension. The prospect of navigating life on a reduced income weighed heavily on her mind, adding another layer of complexity to her grieving process, and causing confusion.

Amid these challenges, the resilience of the human spirit shone through. We clung to each other for support. I knew she would be financially secure, but for her, there was an irritation in her mind that things could have been different.

Thankfully as time passed, Mum got to grips with her finances, and only 12 months later it was her helping me out for money. I have no ego, but it was not a proud moment for an adult who has always been the one looking after everybody else in my life.

I just want to mention again at this point that my home kept me strong and kept me going for everyone else who needed me. Behind my front door lives the two most amazing ladies I could have ever wished for. Ruth isn't much of an emotional talker, but that's perfect, she is a phenomenal listener, and

Danni has a heart bigger than the sun. she is so caring and can bring a smile to soul with just a simple hug.

Chapter 60

The Deposition Dilemma

T he date was January 23rd, 2023, a day etched in my memory as the culmination of months of legal turmoil and uncertainty. It was a journey that had left me restless with nerves, burdened by the weight of an impending legal trial that would determine the course of our lives.

Gary and I embarked on a journey to Atlanta, where our depositions for the legal case awaited us. I had never felt such a profound sense of nervousness and pressure. This was uncharted territory: a whole week of gruelling video depositions that would expose our perspectives, truths, and vulnerabilities to the opposition's legal counsel.

The rules of engagement were clear and unforgiving. We were told to answer only the "exact question" posed to us. If the question was as simple as "Do you know the time?" our response had to be as concise as "yes" or "no." We were to speak only when spoken to and refrain from excessive chatter. This environment demanded discipline and restraint, and words held immense power.

We had to conduct each deposition separately. I went first, but as I sat there listening to Gary's, I couldn't help but reflect on the stark contrast to my usual role. For over 20 years, I have been accustomed to leading meetings, contributing my voice, and participating actively in every discussion. Now,

I found myself in a disempowered position, listening to Gary respond to questions through a wall from the next room.

Inside, I was a tempest of emotions. I was acutely aware of the pressure he was under and the magnitude of the moment. While I couldn't physically be by his side, I was there in spirit, grappling with the questions being posed and the answers being given. It was an agonising experience, feeling out of control and yearning to contribute more than the constraints of the deposition allowed.

Each deposition session followed a gruelling pattern. The opposing counsel would lead us down a winding path of questioning, often for 30 - 45 minutes, before finally arriving at the pivotal, game-changing question. Everything that had been asked before was merely a precursor to this crucial point, a moment of truth that would shape the course of the case.

What I learned about myself during this challenging week was a revelation. It was a testament to the power of habit and the discomfort of relinquishing control. After years of leadership and active participation, listening to Gary respond from the next room was a unique form of torture. I struggled to contain my inner turmoil as I navigated the labyrinth of questions, always mindful of the finality of that critical inquiry.

Gary, for his part, acquitted himself admirably under the intense scrutiny. The opposing counsel sought to turn the screws on him, probing for weaknesses, making arguments that were difficult to refute or disprove. It was a taxing ordeal, and the pressure was palpable.

Lee, on the other hand, took a baffling approach. He claimed not to speak English, a laughable assertion given his long history of dealing with us exclusively in English. He had lived in the United States since the age of 18, held a business degree from UCLA, and his children were fluent English speakers. Lee's propensity for deception extended to every facet of his defence, a testament to the lengths he was willing to go to avoid accountability.

If Lee has an opportunity to lie, he will... and not for any good reason; he is just like that, always has been.

This week of depositions was a crucible, testing our resolve and resilience under immense pressure. It was a pivotal chapter in the legal battle that had come to define our lives. It was horrific.

Chapter 61

The Final Farewell

Two months later, in the midst of our trip to Los Angeles for another ultra-stressful and life-changing legal mediation meeting in Los Angeles, my phone buzzed with an incoming message from Ann, my stepmom. The words on the screen sent a shiver down my spine—it was about Dad's Euthanasia, and the date was set for the following Wednesday, March 15th. A wave of emotions crashed over me, a tumultuous mix of sadness, anxiety, and a profound sense of responsibility.

There was no time to digest this news fully, for we were embroiled in a high-stakes mediation process, one that demanded our unwavering attention that day. Even as we faced the crucible of legal negotiations, the imminent event weighed heavily on my mind. I struggled to concentrate, as I knew what the following few days entailed.

In the middle of this chaos, Dad reached out to me, expressing his wishes regarding the impending euthanasia. He confided that he didn't want Gary to be present at this deeply personal and emotional final moments. I couldn't help but understand his perspective—Gary and Dad had not communicated since our trip to Spain in November (5 months earlier), a silence that had only exacerbated the already strained relationship between them.

It was an emotionally charged dilemma that placed the burden of resolution squarely on my shoulders. Dad's wish was clear, yet I grappled with the decision. The prospect of excluding Gary from such a significant event was difficult to accept, and I believed it was only right for him to be present during Dad's final breath.

I explained to Dad that I wouldn't disclose his request to Gary, understanding that the situation was fraught with tension and complexity. I told him to trust me as I managed it as best I could. As the days unfolded, I found myself navigating the delicate terrain of family dynamics, torn between honouring my father's wishes and the knowledge that this could break Gary for the rest of his life and change a lifetime of memories forever.

Chapter 62

The Night Before

I caught the first possible flight after landing back from LA and touched down in Spain on Tuesday, March 14th, the day before Dad would be visited by the doctors while at home. The weight of the inevitable rested heavily on my shoulders. My sole purpose was to be with Dad and Ann during this poignant moment. Paul, my stepbrother, had also made the journey, a reassuring presence.

Regrettably, Nicola couldn't join us due to her commitments in New Zealand, but she arranged to visit in the following weeks and was always on video with Ann.

The following 24 hours would be among the most emotionally taxing of my life. We all knew that Dad's time was drawing to a close, his decision, but an undeniably strange and solemn experience. Despite the impending sorrow, we chose to cherish the day and evening together. We shared stories, cracked jokes, teased each other, and fondly reminisced about Dad's colourful past. It was a bittersweet day, filled with laughter and tears.

As the clock passed midnight, Gary and I reluctantly left Dad and Ann's side, knowing that the sleepless hours would be spent gazing at the ceiling and grappling with the profound sense of loss that loomed from a nearby hotel bed.

The Spanish night enveloped me as I stepped out into the cool air, the stars above twinkling in silent witness to the emotions that stirred within me. The weight of the impending goodbye hung in the atmosphere, and yet, the shared moments of the day had made me happy, if only for a short time.

Each step to our hotel was silent. I navigated the dimly lit streets in sombre reflection, aware that the next sunrise would herald a new reality.

In the stillness of our lodgings, the magnitude of the situation settled upon me. Sleep proved elusive as each of us grappled with the reality that the dawn would bring both closure and the beginning of a new chapter—one without Dad's physical presence.

As the night unfolded, I found solace in the day we had just shared, knowing that our presence had comforted Dad and Ann during a challenging time. The weight of the inevitable was undeniable, but we faced it together.

Chapter 63

The Final Choice, My Family's Hardest Day

Wednesday, March 15th 2023, arrived, I got dressed in a zombie-like state, my mind filled with a thousand thoughts. Gary and I returned to Dad's side, accompanied by an atmosphere laden with an inexplicable weight. We tried to maintain a light-hearted spirit, honouring Dad's wishes to keep the mood as upbeat as possible. He even requested a simple breakfast—porridge. We all understood the impending reality, but there was nothing more we could do but stand by him.

I remember Dad asking us how our legal battle was going, and Gary and I looking at each other, both confirming that it was nearly over, and we had won. This was clearly not true, but who were we to worry Dad even further at this point. We wanted him to think we were doing OK, and that our families were going to be safe.

But it amazes me that during Dad's final hours, his thoughts were for us, not him. Once a parent, always a parent, I thought.

As the morning unfolded, the nurses arrived just past nine, but Dad requested that they wait. He wasn't quite ready to take that final step. However, as the clock inched toward 10 a.m., he signalled for Ann to call them in. It was then that Ann confided in me—Dad wished for only her and me to be present during his final moments. Gary and Paul would have to leave.

Wow, what a choice to make, but I found myself unable to adhere to Dad's wish. It didn't seem right. I felt that Gary needed to be there more than Dad wanted him out of the room, weighed down by a burdensome guilt that had been growing and intensified by our ongoing legal battle. We had, quite literally, lost everything.

I couldn't. No, sorry. I wouldn't be the person to tell him such a thing.

The nurse and doctor entered the room, and the doctor escorted us outside while the nurse prepared Dad for the procedure. Two injections would mark the transition, the first to quickly halt his breathing, effectively allowing him to pass away, and the second to still his heart forever.

As we waited outside, the doctor explained to us that Dad would be the first person within the vast Valencia region of Spain to undergo this type of procedure, and one of only a couple of people throughout the whole of Spain.

She was clearly living a milestone for her too. Doctors and nurses save lives, not take them. She didn't want to make any mistakes.

As the weight of the moment pressed upon us, the world seemed unusually quiet, the passage of time marked only by the muffled sounds from the room where Dad lay. The decision to have Gary present weighed heavily on my conscience, but it felt like the right choice. In the face of loss, compassion and understanding took precedence over adherence to wishes.

Chapter 64

Pop's Last Breath

Dad occupied his chair, flanked by Ann and the nurse on his left and me and Gary on his right. Ann and I clutched his hands throughout, while Gary stayed by his legs. The gravity of the moment weighed on us all as we understood that this was Dad's final journey, his final goodbye.

As the doctor talked, Dad turned to me, his eyes filled with emotions, and uttered the words that would forever echo in my heart: "Look after my granddaughter." It was a moment that shattered me, that even in his final moments, his thoughts were of Danni.

The doctor asked, "Are you ready, Mike?" Dad replied with a determined "Yes," though a flicker of panic briefly crossed his face—a fleeting, revealing glimpse of his inner thoughts. His ability to communicate had been greatly compromised, leaving him trapped within his body, only sporadically able to convey his thoughts. This was one of those moments.

An hour earlier, we had set up the Alexa to play random music that morning, as the silence was deafening after turning off the TV. Different music filled the room, although nobody was actually listening, until something amazing happened. Something that must have been sent from the afterlife. Just before the nurse knelt down by Dad's side, the room filled with the poignant chords of Eric Clapton's "Tears in Heaven," one of Dad's favourite songs, from his favourite artists. We collectively gasped and experienced a profound moment.

A few seconds later, Dad's breathing ceased, and a serene stillness enveloped him. It was a humbling experience—one of the bravest moments I had ever witnessed, led by the courage of a man who had faced his fate with unwavering resolve.

The young nurse by our side was overcome with tears as we maintained our vigil with Dad until the cremation staff arrived to carry him away. It was a moment of both sorrow and solace, a peaceful farewell to a beloved father who had displayed incomparable bravery in the face of his own mortality.

As the weight of the moment lingered, we found comfort in the shared experience of witnessing Dad's departure. The echoes of his final words and the poignant melody of "Tears in Heaven" resonated within the walls of the room, creating a bittersweet symphony that would forever accompany our memories of that sacred moment of farewell.

Chapter 65

A Final Tribute

Two days after Dad's peaceful passing, on St. Patrick's Day, we gathered to pay our final respects as he was cremated. Eric Clapton's music filled the air, creating a fitting backdrop for a touching service.

Amidst the sombre atmosphere, the warmth of their friends enveloped us. As we stood together, reminiscing about Dad's life and the memories we shared, it was clear that this gathering was a celebration of his legacy. The choice of music, carefully selected to resonate with his spirit, allowed us to find solace amid sorrow.

Many others, unable to attend in person, joined us remotely through the Internet, including Danni and Ruth, while they were at school. The virtual presence of loved ones, even from afar, provided a sense of connection and support. Despite the physical distance, their words of comfort and shared memories reached us, reinforcing the idea that love transcends the boundaries of time and space.

The tree for my Dad, Pops and Brother Mikee

Throughout this turbulent period, Ruth and Danni proved again to be the most incredible family I could have hoped for. Although they faced their own challenges and concerns, we remained united and stronger than ever before.

Ruth's unwavering strength became a pillar of support for all of us. She took on responsibilities with resilience, ensuring that each aspect of Dads farewell reflected Dad's essence.

Meanwhile, Danni's maturity shone through as she navigated the complexities of grief while balancing the demands of school and her GCSE exam year. Her ability to find comfort in routine and stability provided a reassuring anchor for the rest of the family from such a young adult.

Chapter 66

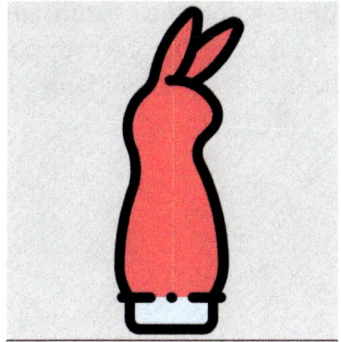

A Haven Called Home

I couldn't ask for a better family life. We've discovered a way of living that works for us, finding strength in togetherness. They are my world, even though Ruth prefers the comfort of home to travel or going out. Our home life is truly wonderful, made even more special by Maggie and Mittens.

In the quiet moments spent within the walls of our home, a sense of peace and contentment prevails. Ruth's preference for the familiar surroundings of our abode has created a haven where love and laughter flourish. While the world outside may be filled with uncertainties, our home remains a sanctuary of stability and warmth.

Danni was preparing for her GCSE exams, scheduled for May and June of that year. She approached each day with remarkable resilience, maintaining her level-headedness, sense of humour, and the positive attitude I had tried to drill into her since a young age at Martial Arts practise.

The academic challenges that lay ahead did little to dim Danni's spirit. Her dedication to her studies, coupled with her ability to find joy in the midst of stress, showcased a maturity beyond her years. As she delved into the intricacies of exam preparation, her commitment to excellence became evident, serving as an inspiration to us all.

Her love for her family and grandparents shines brightly. In just one year, she had faced challenges that most 16-year-olds couldn't fathom, yet her strength and grace stood firm.

As we navigate the complexities of daily life, the small moments within the walls of our home become the most significant. Whether it's a shared meal, a laughter-filled evening, or the quiet support offered during times of study, our home is the backdrop for our family life.

Chapter 67

Rediscovering Life After Loss

Life throws you. Life floors you. But, you know, life also gives you those small chances to get back up and start again. Change is like a constant companion, but so is growth.

One night, sometime after Dad's passing, I sat alone in the dark, contemplating where life would lead me next and what strength I had left to forge ahead. In the face of the grief that follows the loss of a parent (or two,) I discovered a peculiar strength in the ordinary, in the everyday things that persisted.

So, I sat there alone and thought to myself about how I wanted to re-establish my professional life. It was a time of emotional highs and lows, marked by new beginnings. You always hear the saying there's always someone worse off than yourself. It's an important point, but grief doesn't work that way. I knew I could get through this if I put my head down and pushed through.

I was determined to rediscover myself, albeit as a slightly newer version. Life had changed me, I had certainly changed, but it was time to embrace the transformation and move forward.

Chapter 68

Glow Global, My Next Chapter?

For weeks I got exactly nowhere in my thinking — it just all seemed too hard, too complex. I had run too many ideas into a train of intrusive thoughts, and everything went nowhere.

I circulated the issue again and again, threw my hands at it, bashed my head against it...and then one day when I was thinking of nothing much at all, the answer came to me. It arrived whole and complete — gift-wrapped, you could say. I ran home and started sheets upon sheets of planning, because I was terrified of losing the initial idea.

What I saw was the birth of *Glow Global Consulting Ltd*, my little venture back into the business world.

I contacted a few people I had met over the years, offered my assistance, and was given a lifeline by Leon, a guy with charisma to spare. He had these big dreams of growing his business from 60 plus employees to a whopping 200. He was even thinking about taking it public. I thought, "Why not jump in and give it a shot?" It turns out Leon was a bit all over the place. Charismatic, for sure, but reality wasn't his strong suit. Dreaming big is cool, but we were about to find out that dreams and reality don't always align.

I got into the nitty-gritty, working closely with Leon's team in London for a few months.

Sadly, it was a lot of smoke and mirrors. Something was pulling this business one way or the other, and it was starting to fall out of my hands. It turned out he only had two employees in the UK, four on contracts, and twenty developers, all chilling in India. Should've seen this as a red flag, but if you can't change it, you have to deal with it.

All I could do is wait there, look at the sky and listen to my inner optimism telling me I could get through anything.

Even with all the ups and downs, I got along great with Leon's team. We tackled stuff together, and I threw in some cool ideas, especially about using NFC touch technology for art galleries and car dealerships. Trying to keep things fresh.

But in May or June, Leon dropped the bomb. The company was running out of money, and I was out. It hit me hard—I'd just started finding my groove, and now the world was spinning again. I have no shame in admitting it rattled my cage and shook me up.

I was overwhelmed. We had barely scratched the surface, and now it was like hitting a wall. But I had to remember, in the game of life, sometimes you win, sometimes you learn.

Chapter 69

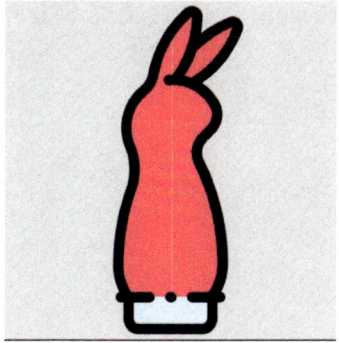

Finding Direction After a Storm

An unwavering thought enters my mind — what comes next?

I squash the thought and meet the eyes of my legal advisor, Ian Wood Smith, my true advisor and one of Southern UK's best lawyers and business advisors. His calmness and advice always make me feel confident again.

I sink into the chair at his reception desk and consider my options, but none of them are ideal. I imagine writing the later chapters of my life story. I wonder if this is how it will be a month or a year from now – one minute, life swims upwards; the next, it takes a tumble; and the next, you just can't be sure.

I keep trying to remind myself. *You've done this dance before. You'll get there again.* It's about reminding myself I've got the skills to navigate the storm and the attitude to overcome anything.

Because every single bone in my body wants to come out on top. Every single one. I want to look after my family again. It's been a tough ride, but I've got to keep driving forward and staying positive. The fight isn't over. Not by a long shot.

Chapter 70

Mittens , Taken Too Soon

Today (January 15th 2024), we said goodbye to Mittens, our Lavender British Shorthair. She's been with us since we first moved into Chaffinch Close, a constant presence as our family grew and changed. Her passing, after twelve years, will leave a quiet space in our home and a loss that will never truly fade.

As the dad, I've always felt it's my job to protect my family from the tough parts of life. But today, I'm grappling with a sense of personal failure, for the first time really. We all know pets don't live as long as we do, but understanding that doesn't seem to make it any easier. I look around at the faces of my family, each one clouded with sadness, and I feel helpless. Our family of five, always so full of laughter and support, will feel incomplete without her. I know I'm not responsible, although, for some reason, I think I am. Such a strange thing to write and feel, but it's the truth. I actually feel I have let our family down.

Mittens was more than just a cat; she was a part of our family's story. Knowing that she got ill and an operation didn't help has hit us all hard. It's tough to see everyone so down, especially knowing there's not much I can do to fix it. In time, will do our best to remember the good times, to smile through the tears. It's not easy, but we're getting there together.

As we navigate this loss, I realise that my role isn't just about shielding my family from sadness but being there with them through it. We're a team – through the highs and the lows. Today, we lost one of our own, and while it hurts more than I can put into words in this book, I know we'll get through it together.

Chapter 71

My Mind Keeps Talking to Me

J an – Feb 2024. After running a fantastic and successful business for
so long, it's tough to come to grips with its loss. That business was
my everyday life, my identity, and I was damn good at it. I stood out in
the adult toy industry, not your typical gig. People respected me in the
industry, and my family and friends admired my success. I never flaunted
wealth with fancy cars or houses, but folks knew I was financially stable
and, more importantly, happy.

But losing my business has affected me more than I ever dreamed possible.
Especially the past six to nine months. My mind's been overwhelmed.
And sleep? Forget it. I can doze off, but by 2–3 a.m., my brain's in high
gear, consumed by anxiety about my uncertain future. My family's future.
Falling back asleep becomes an insurmountable task without some form
of distraction, and more often than not, I find solace in the flickering
glow of the TV. A carefully chosen true crime story programme, selected
specifically as there is rarely any loud noises, and all the conversations are
calm and quiet.

The toll on Ruth has been undeniable, as she's had to retreat to the spare
room to secure even a semblance of rest. After all, she's the one carrying
the weight of our family and household responsibilities.

I'm like a spectator in my own life, distant and disconnected. It's a version of me I've never seen before, struggling to concentrate. I'm doing all I can to stay committed and keep my eye on the future, pushing myself forward. Even without a job to fill my days, I stick to a routine, getting up at 7 a.m., showering, dressing, and taking Maggie for a walk. She's my closest "friend," my comfort in this storm, as I don't need to talk to her about any of the mayhem or worries in my life. She's with me all day, just wanting cuddles and walks. Maggie's my rock, especially as my family, who are amazing, continue with their lives.

Danni, my daughter, is 17 now and thriving. She's an incredible young woman, but she doesn't need her dad as much anymore, and I get that. It makes me happy when I see how capable she is—a little chip off the old block!

I'm certain I'll find my new career soon, maybe back in the adult toy world, which is where my heart still lies. I'm willing to step down a few rungs on the ladder if I join the mainstream, knowing I lack experience in mainstream industries. But right now, with the case due to go to court in a few weeks, the legal case hangs over me, blocking any progress. Every job application asks if I'm currently in a legal case, and my answer is yes, keeping me stuck.

It's a lonely place, this world of legal battles, extortionate costs; personal costs and career ending uncertainty. Only my brother Gary could possibly understand, although we are very different people. We try to support each other, even if we can't fully grasp each other's personal struggles.

Chapter 72

My Chapters of Life: A Journey Through Joy and Adversity

And there's my story so far, the collection of my years. It is the record of a wild ride.

I've had a pretty full life, and I like to think of myself as a profoundly positive and happy person. I've got a great family, awesome friends, and, boy, I've had my fair share of laughs. I'm all about aiming high and chasing success in the future. Life's thrown some challenges my way, but I've always tried to stay positive and keep pushing forward. It's not just about getting by; it's about tackling life head-on.

Family Holiday 1913

I believe that things happen for a reason, even if we can't always figure them out. You just gotta keep on truckin'. And don't forget where you came from and the different versions of yourself that got you here.

What else is there in life if not to share stories?

And oh, to hope that someone might understand and take something from it.

I am, if nothing else, a bundle of chapters and a wealth of experiences.

Before I met Rosie, I was living the bachelor life—fun times, loving life, hanging out with friends, and just having a blast. Money to burn, you know? But life can be a rollercoaster, and I've had my share of ups and downs.

I'm picturing my journey so far, from growing up to imagining myself all old and grey, surrounded by family and friends, reminiscing about the good times. Life ain't over; it's just getting started, and I'm ready to grab every moment.

I've been through some stuff that's left a mark on me, things that not everyone could handle. A few big events have shaped my journey, and I want to share that story. Now, don't get too excited; I won't go into every little detail. I'll save some for the next book. So, reader, I'll talk to you again soon.

Chapter 73

Encore – Has the Curtain Closed?

The countdown to the trial in Los Angeles was a constant weight on my mind, even as life continued with other challenges. Every conversation with Gary, every sleepless night, was underscored by the looming uncertainty. The trial wasn't just about business—it was about our reputations, our livelihoods, and the future we had worked so hard to build. Yet, life had a way of throwing curveballs, and the months leading up to the trial were anything but straightforward.

Navigating the Job Market and Finding New Opportunities

Following our return from California in February 2024, I found myself adrift, grappling with the dual pressures of an unresolved legal case and the urgent need to secure a new role. I dedicated nearly all my time to the job search, refining my CV and applying for roles that aligned with my skills. But the job market was a tough nut to crack. My experience as a business owner was a double-edged sword: while it showcased my versatility and leadership, many employers viewed my entrepreneurial background with suspicion.

Initially, I aimed for high-level positions such as Chief Operations Officer (COO) or Strategy Director. Yet, it quickly became clear that these roles were either filled internally or by industry insiders with more mainstream corporate backgrounds. Undeterred, I pivoted to focus on product management roles, a field where my passion for innovation could shine. By May, this change in strategy began to bear fruit, leading to several promising interviews.

One role, in particular, stood out: Product Manager at Stuart Turner Ltd., a respected name in water pump solutions. After a series of interviews, I was thrilled to receive an offer in late June. It felt like a turning point—a chance to apply my experience in a new industry, while building a stable future for my family. This marked the start of an exciting new chapter.

Trials on and off the Pitch

Amid the job search, another challenge loomed—this time, a physical one. In April 2024, during a routine football match, I suffered a significant injury to my left hip. At the time, I shook it off, thinking it was just another knock. But as the pain persisted, I knew something was wrong. After months of physiotherapy and specialist consultations, I was diagnosed with arthritis in both hips, compounded by a condition known as CAM hip.

The news was sobering. My years of intense physical activity—football, martial arts, and gym sessions—had taken their toll, and I was now facing the prospect of dual hip replacements. However, a specialist suggested an alternative: a hip arthroscopy to repair the damage and delay the need for full replacements. The surgery was scheduled for July 15, just days before starting my new role at Stuart Turner Ltd.

The Surgery and a Life-Altering Goodbye

On the morning of July 15th, I woke early, my stomach in knots. Despite my nerves, I took comfort in the fact that Mr. Andrade, one of the UK's top hip surgeons, would be performing the procedure. After kissing Ruth and Danni goodbye, I headed to Harley Street. But before I left, I felt compelled to write them a note. It wasn't something I'd done before, but the idea of going under the knife had stirred something deep inside me. In that letter, I told them how much I loved them, that they should stay strong and look after each other no matter what. I made sure to mention Malcolm and Martin, two trusted friends who managed our savings and insurance, just in case things didn't go as planned.

Lying on the bed in the sedation room, the medical team reassured me the procedure would take two to three hours. I was even told I'd be awake in time to watch the Euro semi-finals that evening. But when I finally came round, shivering under heated blankets, I realized things hadn't gone as smoothly as expected. Mr. Andrade entered the room, his expression a mix of relief and concern.

"The operation went well," he began, "but the damage to your hip was far worse than we anticipated. The surgery took nearly six hours because of the additional work required. Unfortunately, this procedure is only a temporary fix—you'll still need a full hip replacement, and likely within the next one to five years."

It was another blow, another challenge to face. But what hit hardest wasn't just the physical recovery—it was the reality that my days of playing football, something I'd loved since childhood, were likely over. Football had always been more than a sport for me. It was a way to connect with friends, clear my mind, and feel like part of something bigger. Letting go of that part of my life felt like losing an old friend.

Despite this, I knew I couldn't dwell on the loss. My new role at Stuart Turner Ltd. awaited, and the court case still loomed. I resolved to tackle each challenge with the same resilience that had carried me through every other storm. Life might throw its curveballs, but I've learned to hit them back with persistence and a positive attitude.

As I often remind myself: only I can get up every morning and make the best of the day ahead. Only I can ensure my family stays safe and secure.

Chapter 74

Encore's Encore

I never expected there to be two Encore chapters, but after the second postponement of our trial in nine months, I wanted to finish with the actual trial. So please hold that wee for another few minutes—we're nearly at the conclusion, good or bad.

The final court trial date was set for the end of October 2024. Leading up to it, my emotions were on a rollercoaster. Mentally, it was tough, especially with Gary not speaking to me. I understood that the pressure of what was happening weighed heavily on us both, but it didn't make those silent months any easier. I was hopeful it was just a phase, something that would pass once the trial was behind us. Still, it added a layer of stress I'd gladly forget forever.

Pre-Trial Jitters and Family Moments

Two weeks before the trial, I could feel the familiar tension creeping in—sleepless nights, a restless mind, and an ever-growing list of responsibilities. At Stuart Turner, I was fully immersed in a major Strategy project, working closely with the Managing Director and CEO. It was a 'new' career-defining opportunity, but balancing this with the impending trial was no small feat. Each day, I pushed myself to give 100% at work, and each night, I found myself staring at the ceiling, the weight of the trial pressing down on me.

Then came a night I'll never forget. It was the Thursday before I was set to fly to LA. Feeling the full weight of stress but determined not to let it affect my family, I invited Danni out to quiz night at The Fox. "Fancy it?" I asked her, and to my delight, she jumped at the chance. Teaming up with Daryl, Ollie, and Danni under the name "Three Men and a Little Lady," we set out to have a laugh. But life had other plans.

Midway through the quiz, Ruth called in tears. "Something's wrong with Dad," she said in a panic. "Get here now." I bolted home, leaving Danni with the guys, and we rushed to Theale to find Roger slumped in bed, struggling to speak to the 999 operator. Linda was in a panic, and I quickly took over. Despite Roger's insistence that he was fine, I knew better and demanded an ambulance.

Minutes later, the paramedics arrived. As they climbed the stairs, I explained Roger's alarming state—only for them to find him sitting upright, looking much improved. "Hi Roger, I'm Owen," one paramedic said, but before he could continue, Roger interjected, "Knock, knock." Confused, Owen played along: "Who's there?" "Owen," Roger replied, then burst into song: "Oh when the Saints, go marching in!" It was classic Roger.

The paramedics suspected a mini-stroke or stress, likely triggered by the sudden passing of Uncle Don earlier that week – a family legend of Ruth's someone who grew up as close as a brother to Roger.

We returned home, only to learn our quiz team had come last—beaten by Steve, who had survived a severe brain injury decades earlier – they clearly missed me! . That night, I caught myself spiraling, overwhelmed by everything: the trial, family health, and my strained relationship with Gary. But as I stared into the bathroom mirror, something clicked. "You've got this," I told myself. And just like that, a wave of calm washed over me.

The Courtroom Drama

Walking into the Federal Courtroom in Downtown LA was surreal. The grandeur of the room, with its high ceilings, polished wood, and rows of perfectly arranged seats, was intimidating yet awe-inspiring. It felt like stepping onto the set of a Hollywood legal drama. But this wasn't a movie—it was real. Our two-and-a-half-year battle had brought us here, to one of the most significant courtrooms in America.

Federal Court Los Angeles

This was the same courtroom where the infamous Rodney King case was tried in the early '90s, a trial that ignited nationwide protests and became a pivotal moment in the fight against police brutality. The weight of that history wasn't lost on me. The thought of all the high-stakes cases that had played out in this very room made our own trial feel monumental.

The stakes couldn't have been higher. Everything we'd fought for—our business, our reputations, and our financial future—was now in the hands of a jury. As I took my seat, I reminded myself that this wasn't just about winning or losing; it was about vindicating the truth.

Day one began with jury selection, an exhausting process that felt more like theatre than justice. Lee's attorney, Doug, pulled every trick in the book, even asking jurors if they thought James Bond was "debonair" to gauge their bias towards Brits. It was laughable, but the gravity of the situation was never lost on me.

The following days were a whirlwind of opening statements, testimonies, and sidebars. Lee's team painted a picture of us as schemers who owed him $2.6 million, twisting facts to fit their narrative. What hit hardest was watching Lee, a man who had communicated perfectly in English for over two decades, had an International Business degree from a Los Angeles University, suddenly require an interpreter. It was absurd, but we had no choice but to endure. Put it this way, Gary nor I can speak any Mandarin apart from ordering a beer!

By Thursday, it was my turn on the stand. Surprisingly, I felt calm. For the first time in days, I woke up energized. I knew my life story and responsibilities inside out. My only job was to tell the truth and keep it simple. As I sat there, answering questions and cross-examinations, I felt like I was back in my element. I even found myself in front of a large white board, explaining how I created collections and Patented products while also sketching out ideas for new product designs during the breaks. This was my world, and Lee's lawyers had no chance against me.

Our witnesses, Derek and Geoff, played a crucial role in reinforcing our credibility, but their significance extended far beyond the courtroom. Derek, a trusted collaborator for years, was not just a colleague; he was a friend who understood my vision and creativity. On the stand, he spoke with conviction about our work together, especially on projects like Pure Romance, calling me "one of the most innovative and talented people" he'd ever worked with.

His words hit me hard, not because I doubted myself, but because they validated everything I'd fought to protect.

Then there was Geoff Mesher, our forensic accountant. A no-nonsense numbers guy with a wicked sense of humour, Geoff had spent months dissecting financial records to prepare our case. On the stand, he was methodical and unshakable, the perfect counter to the other side's claims. Off the stand, he was a character. On the eve of the trial, he celebrated his birthday at a LA Rams game, only to show up the next day with a bruised and scratched forehead and a tale of a late-night whisky bar detour. That's Geoff—sharp as a tack and always keeping things light when the pressure was on. These two weren't just professional allies; they were reminders that the people you surround yourself with can make or break you in tough times.

Verdict Day

Friday came too quickly, and with it, the closing statements that would seal our fate. As both legal teams made their final cases, I couldn't help but feel the weight of everything that had brought us to this moment. The trial wasn't just about financial restitution; it was about our integrity, our legacy, and proving that we had always operated with honesty. As the jury retired to deliberate, the waiting game began.

What followed was agonizing. The jury took the entire weekend to reach their decision, each passing hour stretching endlessly. Every time my phone buzzed, my heart leapt, only to realize it wasn't the call. I replayed the trial in my head repeatedly—every argument, every witness testimony. I could only hope the jury saw through Lee's charade and recognized the truth we had laid bare.

The hardest part was having to leave LA before the verdict. Monday morning arrived, and duty called. I boarded the flight back to the UK, weighed down by nerves and the knowledge that I wouldn't be there in person to hear the jury's decision. By the time I touched down and returned to work at Stuart Turner, my mind was still thousands of miles away in that Los Angeles courtroom.

Monday dragged on at a snail's pace. My new role demanded focus, but my thoughts were elsewhere. Every tick of the clock seemed louder, every moment without news stretched unbearably. By evening, I was back home, pacing the living room like a man waiting outside the delivery room.

And then, at last, my phone buzzed. It was a video call from Gary. I froze for a second, the weight of anticipation crashing down on me. As I answered, his face appeared, lit with sheer elation.

"WE WON!" he shouted, unable to contain his excitement. Behind him, our lawyers—David, Jeff, and Brandon—were grinning from ear to ear. Gary's voice was trembling with disbelief and joy. "It was a complete whitewash. We won on every single count. The jury believed us over Lee on everything! They've awarded us $9 million!"

It took a moment for the words to sink in. And then, like a dam breaking, the floodgates opened. Tears streamed down my face as two and a half years of pent-up emotion—stress, frustration, hope, and sheer exhaustion—poured out. The victory wasn't about the money, though that would undoubtedly help secure our future. It was about vindication. We had fought for the truth, and the truth had prevailed.

The jury had seen through every falsehood, every exaggerated claim, every desperate attempt by Lee's team to paint us as the villains. They believed in us, in our story, in the evidence we had worked so hard to present. It was a clean sweep—a unanimous decision that validated everything we stood for.

That night, I called Danni first. She had been anxiously waiting, so nervous she'd gone out to grab a McFlurry to calm her nerves. Her excitement matched mine as I told her the news. Then I called Mum, followed by my old-school lads. I wanted to share the moment with everyone who had supported me through this journey. But after those calls, I took a moment to myself, letting the victory sink in fully.

This trial had tested us in every possible way—our business, our reputations, even the bond between Gary and me as brothers. But we'd emerged from the storm stronger, vindicated, and ready to move forward. The truth had won, and in that moment, I felt lighter than I had in years.

Then, just as I was settling into the glow of victory, my phone buzzed again. It was Gary, and his tone was more subdued this time. "Mate, there's been a bit of a mix-up," he said. My heart skipped a beat. "The actual award is $8.4 million—not $9 million. There was a mistake on the form." In the span of an hour, we'd lost $600,000. I let out a laugh, more amused than annoyed. "Oh well," I said. "We'll just have to make do." After everything we'd been through, what was another twist in the tale? The real victory wasn't in the number—it was in proving ourselves and clearing our name.

Closing Reflection

This chapter, this trial, was about more than just money or business. It was about standing firm in the face of injustice, about resilience, and about the unshakable belief that the truth would prevail.

The fight isn't over—there will be appeals, legal formalities, and battles yet to come. But for now, I can hold my head high, proud of what we've achieved. Life is unpredictable, but if there's one thing I've learned, it's this: when you stay true to yourself and those you love, you can weather any storm.

Acknowledgements

I am grateful to everyone who has helped and supported me along the way.

To my family, and my friends, thank you for your patience, your generosity, your warmth and you're understanding. Thank you for believing in me all the way through. Thank you for allowing me to push myself; life has been far more interesting.

Every day is different.

And so, thank you, reader, and look out for part two.

A Special Message to Danni

Danni – My World, travelling buddy and best friend. When I'm gone, I want you to remember ALL of our time together, every holiday, every car journey, every day we spent together that you remember. I want you to talk about every memory as much as possible and be happy. You gave me the happiest moments in my whole life, and I want them to live on forever. Don't ever feel bad about remembering the good times... good memories should be passed on forever. I won't be here forever, but I live on in you. Never forget that.

Printed in Dunstable, United Kingdom